WHAT IS A BOOK?
Thoughts About Writing

WHAT is a BOOK?

THOUGHTS ABOUT WRITING

BY

FRANCES LESTER WARNER · ELLEN GLASGOW · RAFAEL SABATINI · GERTRUDE ATHERTON · HAVELOCK ELLIS MARY AGNES HAMILTON · JEANETTE EATON · HAROLD NICOLSON · VALENTINE WILLIAMS · PHYLLIS BOTTOME GEORGE FORT MILTON · EDWARD J. O'BRIEN · FRANCES FROST · ARCHIBALD MACLEISH · HERBERT AGAR · MARGARET AYER BARNES · ESTHER FORBES · E. ARNOT ROBERTSON · JAMES NORMAN HALL · JOHN LIVINGSTON LOWES

Edited by DALE WARREN

Essay Index Reprint Series

BOOKS FOR LIBRARIES PRESS
FREEPORT, NEW YORK

First Published 1935
Reprinted 1972

Library of Congress Cataloging in Publication Data

Warren, Dale, 1897- ed.
  What is a book?

  (Essay index reprint series)
  Reprint of the 1935 ed.
  Bibliography: p.
  1. Authorship--Addresses, essays, lectures.
2. Literature--Addresses, essays, lectures.
I. Warner, Frances Lester, 1888- II. Title
PN149.W35   1972   808'.02   70-90690
ISBN 0-8369-2875-X

PRINTED IN THE UNITED STATES OF AMERICA

For
'RAFFLES'

PUBLISHERS' NOTE

What is a book?

A book's a book, retorted Mary Lamb, and that was the end of it.

One editor at least is inclined to disagree, and those whose convictions are recorded in the following pages likewise appear to believe that the question cannot be answered so simply.

The present volume is addressed, not primarily to the writer — embryonic or mature — but to the general reader; for realistically viewed, a book, as R. L. Duffus has quite fitly observed, is only one half of an equation, of which the other half is the individual who is reading it.

DALE WARREN

CONTENTS

I.	OF WRITING BOOKS. By *Frances Lester Warner*	3
II.	HEROES AND MONSTERS. By *Ellen Glasgow*	15
III.	HISTORICAL FICTION. By *Rafael Sabatini*	23
IV.	WANTED: IMAGINATION. By *Gertrude Atherton*	43
V.	THE ARTIST IN WORDS. By *Havelock Ellis*	63
VI.	THE WILL TO WRITE. By *Mary Agnes Hamilton*	79
VII.	OUR MOST EXACTING AUDIENCE. By *Jeanette Eaton*	97
VIII.	HOW I WRITE BIOGRAPHY. By *Harold Nicolson*	107
IX.	ON CRIME FICTION. By *Valentine Williams*	119
X.	THE RESPONSIBILITIES OF A WRITER. By *Phyllis Bottome*	133
XI.	HISTORY AS A MAJOR SPORT. By *George Fort Milton*	147
XII.	THE AMERICAN SHORT STORY. By *Edward J. O'Brien*	163
XIII.	THE ETERNAL APPRENTICE. By *Frances Frost*	179
XIV.	EMOTION AND FORM IN POETRY. By *Archibald MacLeish*	187
XV.	JUST WHY ECONOMICS. By *Herbert Agar*	193
XVI.	THE PERIOD NOVEL. By *Margaret Ayer Barnes*	213
XVII.	WHY THE PAST? By *Esther Forbes*	223
XVIII.	ON ANSWERING QUESTIONS. By *E. Arnot Robertson*	237
XIX.	CACOËTHES SCRIBENDI. By *James Norman Hall*	249
XX.	OF READING BOOKS. By *John Livingston Lowes*	261
	LIST OF PUBLICATIONS	289

ANATOLE FRANCE

What is a book? A series of little printed signs — essentially only that. It is for the reader to supply himself the forms and colors and sentiments to which these signs correspond. It will depend on him whether the book be dull or brilliant, hot with passion or cold as ice. Or, if you prefer to put it otherwise, each word in a book is a magic finger that sets a fiber of our brain vibrating like a harp-string, and so evokes a note from the sounding-board of our soul. No matter how skillful, how inspired, the artist's hand; the sound it wakes depends on the quality of the strings within ourselves.

FRANCES LESTER WARNER
discourses on butter-and-eggs, conducts an orchestra, and proffers a 'tuffet' to Mr. Henry James.

OF WRITING BOOKS

YOU could tell by the sound of tearing paper that Tyler had started to write. You could tell by the sound of crumpling paper that he was beginning to get on. His troubles might not have advanced beyond the waste-basket stage, to be sure; but there was a real difference between the disease symptomized by tearing, and that of crumpling.

A little later, you could tell that Tyler had commenced to turn out something suitable for his publishers, by the fact that he began to kick the loose slat down from the under side of his desk. He kept the slat there to brace his feet on in moments of excitement. But so precarious was its balance that when stepped upon without consideration, it fell off. Each time the crash came, Tyler, still absorbed in composition, would fish down with his long arm and replace the slat. Urged on by a rapid rhythm of propping and kicking, his writing would advance. Therefore, in moments of really successful authorship, he sounded from a distance like the most mettlesome horse in a racing-stable, trying to kill his groom.

At such an hour, it was not over-safe to go too near. Authors vary in technique, even within themselves. But, generally speaking, the only point in the writer's working day when Tyler definitely thirsted for communion from outside was the moment when he had just received a letter of acceptance from an editor. Out of his work-room he would prance, his hair on end, his existence justified. Here was the high peak for exalted friendship, for celebration — and for new ideas.

On one such jubilant morning, he had rounded up all the standers-by to drive with him into a sparsely settled region, for a visit to a colonial homestead that had been the hiding-place of one of the country's early alchemists. As we drove through the sunny countryside, we approached the most flourishing field of yellow-flowered black mustard that I had ever seen. The canary-colored blossoms of the mustard grew so thickly that the entire level of the meadow was frothed up high with yellow, almost to the top bar of the wooden fence. And poised above that fluttering cloth of gold, a black-and-yellow bobolink was in full song.

'Look at that field of butter-and-eggs!' Tyler exclaimed to me in a hasty aside, and then turned back to general conversation with the group.

For an instant, I wondered whether I ought to set him right. But I had been trained by a father who allowed himself a comfortable latitude in the use of botanical terms. If he saw a pond blue with the spires of pickerel-weed, for instance, he liked to be able to say benignly, 'Take a good look at those unusual wild blue water-hyacinths,' without risk of being corrected. Perhaps Tyler would feel the same about his butter-and-eggs. Who was I to obtrude a pedantic matter of black mustard (*brassica nigra*) into a blue-and-golden morning of bobolinks and good cheer?

But next day, Tyler's secretary came to me in distress, with a page of a new chapter that she had been asked to type. And there, confronting me accusingly, was a vivid glorification of butter-and-eggs — acres of it — clouds of it — tall plants with lacy racemes of dainty petals borne in airy clusters, all in one clear hue of palest yellow, spilling out over the fence-rails in delicate showers.

'I told him,' said the secretary, 'that I didn't *think* a field of butter-and-eggs would look like that. But he said you saw it, and that I was to go and ask you.'

My only possible answer was to lend Tyler my copy of Gray's field manual, marked in two places with narrow paper slips. On one of these book-marks I had drawn a little spray of mustard; and on the other, in two contrasting shades of yellow crayon, I had sketched a snapdragon-shaped blossom of butter-and-eggs, with an apologetic expression around its drooping mouth.

Ever since that remorseful day, I have treated the entire mental and visual apparatus of all writers with tender care. You can never tell from the looks of an author when he may be taking in material for his work. The writing of a book can involve the complete waking and sleeping life — with time out for doldrums, perhaps, but even the doldrums made significant with a sense of things to come. Sailors in the doldrums talk about the 'brewing' of the wind. There is precisely some such mysterious off-horizon witch-work of the elements for which the becalmed author sometimes has to wait.

What he does while he waits depends upon his degree of desperation, upon the date at which his manuscript has been promised, and upon his disposition.

'Now, on the NINTH OF THE MONTH,' wails Mr.

Charles Dickens in a letter to a friend, 'I have not written a single slip. My wretchedness is inconceivable.... You know my state of mind as well as I do; indeed, if you don't know it much better, it is not the state of mind I take it to be. How I work, how I walk, how I shut myself up, how I roll down hills and climb up cliffs; how the new story is everywhere — heaving in the sea, flying with the clouds, blowing with the wind; how I settle to nothing, and wonder in the old way at my own incomprehensibility.'

And Thackeray, just before writing 'The Newcomes,' is even more deeply in despair: 'Yesterday I sat for six hours and could do no work; I wasn't sentimentalizing but I couldn't get the pen to go. It seems to me that I have said my say, as if everything I write must be repetition, and that people will say with justice, "He has worn himself out — I always told you he would." The days keep dashing on and now it is Tuesday again, and in a few minutes it will be Wednesday, and I am in a ceaseless whirl, yet can get nothing done. I have had a bad week, and a most cruel time of it. My groans were heart-rending, and my sufferings immense.'

Samuel Butler, under similar urgencies of novel-writing, used to go into the British Museum, find a particular large flat book in a special place in the stacks, use it for a lap-board, and write upon it with steady inspiration. But, alas, one day, somebody drew out the large flat book; whereupon Samuel Butler could not for a long time get any writing done.

Mrs. Atherton, unable to get started on an international novel she had promised once upon a time, offered prayer as a last resort at the French shrine of Bonsecours — a notably unconventional 'address to the Almighty,' which began with the earnest words, 'Look here!'

Mark Twain went to bed to write, and so, perforce, did Stevenson. Thoreau took to the woods. Dr. Holmes prowled around Boston. Hawthorne went up into his roof-top study through a trap-door, and drew up the ladder after him. Mrs. Meynell wrote her exquisite prose with half a dozen of her children under her writing-table, editing an amateur magazine of their own. 'Any place will do,' said Louisa Alcott; 'a pad of paper and an atlas on my knee.' And Henry James used to talk out his perplexities while an amanuensis faithfully took them down, whenever he was groping for an idea.

One of his most amazing monologues of this kind, that his amanuensis has preserved for us, is his soliloquy about his novel, 'The Sense of the Past,' that unfinished story which John Balderston recently dramatized as 'Berkeley Square.' It appears that Henry James originally had an idea for one part of that story which he never wrote down, and consequently forgot. 'I seem,' he dictates reflectively to his amanuensis, 'to have intended somehow, in my original view, an accident, a complication, a catastrophic perversity or fatality, as it were, through which Ralph has addressed himself first to the elder, the wrong sister — and when I try to recover what I had in my head about this, there glimmers out, there floats shyly back to me from afar, the sense of something like this, a bit difficult to put — and that as I catch hold of the tip of the tail of it yet again strikes me as adding to my action but another admirable twist. Of course I am afraid of twists — I mean of their multiplying on my hands to the effect of too much lengthening and sprawling ——'

There is much to be learned from this. If Henry James could forget, 'as it were,' what he was going to say — so can we! Every writer should have a handy covert where he can hastily jot down some brimming phrase or sudden impetus of thought before it is too late. There is one busy writer who has solved this problem by means of a vast Victorian pincushion that she inherited from an aunt. That satin pincushion is almost as large as a hassock — exactly one's childhood notion of the 'tuffet' that Miss Muffet sat upon. It is kept on an accessible yet not too conspicuous shelf, with a paper of pins at one side of it, and a pile of paper-slips on the other side. When a sudden idea befalls its owner, she repairs to her pincushion, scribbles the idea on one of the slips of paper, and impales it on the cushion with a pin. Then when she is ready to write, instead of turning the pages of a notebook, or emptying out the items from a large manila envelope, or sorting the contents of a filing-cabinet — she simply takes down her pincushion and gazes at it, as an astronomer might gaze upon a planet, until she spies the very idea she is searching for, fluttering before her on its little pole. The advantages of this plan are obvious to anybody who has ever seen that satin cushion bristling with plots, with local color, with traits and names for characters, and with extra pins.

This business of quickly nailing down each bit of impromptu wording as it comes to mind is perhaps more useful to the writer of books of essays than to anybody else; because the essay in its nature comes the nearest to spontaneous talk. The essayist does not have to adapt his thought to the exigencies of suspense, as in the novel, or of the footlights, as in a play. He comes out to talk with us by his own firelight, in the manner of Dr. Crothers with his 'Gentle Reader'; or drenched with the drizzle of his own rainy twilights, like Bliss Perry in his 'Fishing with a Worm.' Conversationally he brings his personal adventures into the circle of our reading-lamp, with whatever random comments may occur to him: as in Lord Grey's essay on 'Recreation'; or B. K. Hart's ineffable study of the Skunk Cabbage, 'the cleanest and most well-washed little fellow in the world, yet nobody ever asks him to the house a second time'; or Dallas Lore Sharp's 'Turtle Eggs for Agassiz'; or John Burroughs's rare treatise on 'The Wit of a Duck.'

Talking with us at their leisure, venturing their whole personalities for the sake of coming before us conversationally, intimately, as friends among friends, the master essayists of three centuries have developed a most civilized and infinitely flexible prose-pattern for us as they have gone along. But by very reason of this highly personal and communicative quality of the essay, the writer of a complete volume of them is likely to suffer some agitated moments until his book is published and favorable reviews come in. The most exuberant 'familiar essayist' in the world, after laying himself open to criticism by publishing his thoughts, will always have a tendency to grow introspective, subdued, and very grim about himself at times. Once and for all, Michel de Montaigne has put the sensation into words. The remark occurs in one of his confidential descriptions about his own writing ways. 'Sometimes,' says the great Montaigne modestly, after recounting several other matters of intimate technique, 'sometimes I greatly mistrust myself, and shake my ears.'

The trade-malady of the essayist is not writers' cramp; it is an occasional acute attack of shaking at the ears.

And speaking of causes for shaking and quaking, I have been asked to include, somewhere in this discussion, a first-hand account of how I wrote something of my own. I have chosen for this purpose the first chapter of my first book, a sketch of an amateur orchestra, because it was the most predominantly social of all my attempts at writing, and therefore the most pleasant to describe.

Our whole family had assembled for reunion on a certain Christmas vacation. We had spent the first evening playing all the old favorites we ever knew. And on Saturday morning, the three cooks of the family, my mother, my sister, and I, were assembled in the big kitchen concocting traditional foods. Our kitchen-quarters were the dream palace of all ardent cooks, comprising not only a roomy space for working, but sundry little cubicles adjoining — the sort of tiny extra pantry that the Frenchwoman calls 'l'office.' I was in one of these, with my entire 'batterie de cuisine,' perfecting an orange pudding. My sister was in the next cell, mixing cake. The colored maid-of-all-work, little Dimity, was washing our cooking-dishes as fast as we sent them out. Our mother, cutting cookies at a central table, called in impartially to us, 'Some day one of you ought to write about our experiments with a family orchestra. You could use things that happened last night — when Geoffrey tripped over his music-stand and fell into the work-basket, for instance, and when he roared "Three Flats." '

At these words I left my beaten egg-whites in their furrow, and looked out at my pantry door. 'Yes,' said I, 'and when you and Father said "Repeat" and "Don't repeat" at the same instant ——'

'If you think you can write it,' said my sister, slipping her cake into the oven, 'I'll gladly finish your pudding.'

Not a person present, not even Dimity at the saucepans, accused me of taking advantage of an 'escape mechanism' when I vanished up the stairs. They all knew that I would far rather brown the méringue on my pudding in pleasant company than go upstairs into chilly exile to write my piece. From time to time — one sharp pencil in my right hand and four sharp pencils in my left — I would dart down the back stairway to the landing, and read what I had written, blackly interlined and footnoted, on my big ruled pad. Each installment of reading brought me new suggestions from the orchestra circle, and back up the stairway I would scud, my pencils pointing right onward as I ran.

Whenever I write, I depend, with an almost superstitious reliance, upon my extra fagot of pencils for support. The mere possession of so many sharpened pencils gives me a sense of wealth and great resource. And besides, they are a great aid to mental balance if tightly gripped. I like them because they provide something to hold on to — much as a tight-rope walker likes to hold a parasol in his 'slide for life.' And so, vibrating between my room and the back-stairs landing, I paced off the opening measures of my orchestra chapter that snowy Saturday morning, and stayed at home from church to finish it next day.

On Sunday afternoon, I corralled my mother and sister, and read them the rough draft. When we had concluded our discussion of specific alterations, my mother fired a depth-bomb by announcing that one of my pages as I had written it sounded a trifle flat; and that I'd better not even try to improve it, but substitute something entirely different instead.

Keyed up with excitement and hard labor, I took umbrage at this remark, and assured my mother in no uncertain terms that she disliked the passage because it was the only page that did not mention our family. Not at all affrighted by this broadside, she stood firm. I departed in a blaze of fireworks, and spent my spare minutes for the next few days re-writing the whole thing. This time I dealt with the material as if I were my mother speaking, viewing the group through her eyes, commenting with her voice. There was an immense advantage in this, because she could call my father by his first name; and, as 'Endicott,' he assumed his rightful personality at the piano, improvising little trills and arpeggios while we tried to tune our instruments, and refusing to play five sharps. I entitled the chapter 'Endicott and I Conduct an Orchestra,' wound it up with an entirely new conclusion, and the family inspectors released it with very little change.

Of course, my sort of essay-writing is extremely 'light' — the lighter-than-air craft of the literary world. My culminating problem is what Tyler calls the 'terminational terror' — the problem of getting my free balloon down to a fairly respectable landing. In a real balloon, it is easy to tell whether you have landed without destroying your cargo or losing your passengers; but in your writing, until your critics have reported, you can never be quite sure. With books of my own, therefore, when they are supposed to be finished, I try an experiment that I learned long ago from Tyler. After his writing has had a chance to cool off, he reads it over many times, pretending to himself that he is a different reader every time. First he reads it, 'being' his favorite editor. Then he reads it, 'being' his most skeptical friend. And once he brought a manuscript to me and begged me to read it, 'being' Alexander Woollcott.

But there is a 'ceiling' to the imaginative flights that are safe for human kind. In spite of our shrewd surmises, and in spite of our efforts to project ourselves into an outside judgment, the individual response of any particular person will always be a tantalizing enigma that forever baffles us, forever leads us on. In each new generation, the ultimate art of stirring the reader must freshly be explored. That is one reason why there will probably be no end — as long as anybody in the world knows how to read — of writing books.

WILLIAM FAULKNER

I write when the spirit moves me, and it moves me almost every day.

JULIA PETERKIN

I find that my ideas flow most freely when it is too hot to breathe.

T. S. STRIBLING

The reason for the recent literary renaissance in the South is that the heat makes everyone sleepy, and when a writer is sleepy he can most easily get his subconscious working.

REBECCA WEST

The lives of bankers are a hundred times more adventurous and daring than those of writers.

TURGENEV

My publisher keeps circling round me like an eagle, screaming for something.

ARNOLD BENNETT

The novelist should cherish and burnish the faculty of seeing crudely, simply, artlessly, ignorantly; of seeing like a baby or a lunatic, who lives each moment by itself and tarnishes the present by no remembrance of the past.

> ELLEN GLASGOW *warns us that the literature which crawls too long in the mire will soon lose the power of standing erect.*

HEROES AND MONSTERS

THIRTY years ago, I objected to the evasive idealism in American novels. Nowadays, I object to the aimless violence. Not that I oppose either evasiveness or violence as material for fiction, provided the whole cloth is not cut, as dressmakers say, on the bias, and draped round a lay figure in a uniform style. But whenever I watch the professional rebels against gentility basking in that lurid light so fashionable at present among the genteel, I remember with a smile the local thunder-storm that followed my first modest effort to overturn a literary convention.

Thus it occurs to me that the flavor of plain truth, culled from long and sometimes bitter experience, may not be unwholesome today. For of all the weeds that grow and run wild in Southern soil, plain truth is the most difficult to serve without sauce. Moreover, there does not exist in the South today, nor has there ever existed at any time, a treatment of truth in fiction so plain and broad that it could be called, with fairness, a school of realism. There are, no doubt, a few scattered realists, as lonely as sincerity in any field, who dwell outside the Land of Fable inhabited by fairies and goblins. But goblins are as unreal as fairies; and beneath the red paint and charcoal, Raw-Head-and-Bloody-Bones is our battered old friend, Jack-the-Giant-Killer. We remain incurably romantic. Only a puff of smoke separates the fabulous Southern hero of the past from the fabulous Southern monster of the present — or the tender dreams of James Lane Allen from the fantastic nightmares of William Faulkner.

So I shall pass on while I toss a magnolia blossom to those intrepid novelists who have won fine Southern reputations in the North — the only climate, it appears, that has ever been favorable to Southern literary reputations. To confine myself to a few of the notable successes of the year, I congratulate Eleanor Carroll Chilton, Elizabeth Madox Roberts, Thomas Wolfe, William Faulkner, Berry Fleming, Hamilton Basso. I welcome Stark Young's glowing reaffirmation of courage in defeat. I salute Douglas Southall Freeman's superb life of Lee, which has restored not only pure biography to English letters, after a period of wild oats and light living, but even the obsolete word 'duty' to the American tongue. And nothing, I am persuaded, except perhaps a recovered faith in Santa Claus, could confer greater happiness on a liberated world than the miraculous resurrection of the sense of duty. In a sultry age, when we need the tonic of a bracing literature, character has become a lost quantity in fiction, and we miss the full, clear, commanding note of the disciplined mind. Our very vocabulary whines or blusters.

Turning from the formal traditions in Mr. Young's book, which is more sound history than sheer romance, to the inflamed rabble of impulses in the contemporary Southern novel, one asks immediately: What is left of the pattern? Has Southern life — or is it only Southern fiction — become one vast, disordered sensibility? Is there no Southern horizon beyond Joyce? Where is that 'immoderate past' celebrated in Allen Tate's loyal 'Ode to the Confederate Dead'; has 'the salt of their blood' oozed away in a flicker of iridescent scum on the marshes? Does defeat always appear nobler than victory? Or is the whole tedious mass production of degeneracy in our fiction — the current literary gospel of futility and despair — merely a single symptom of the neuroses inflicted on its slaves by the conquering dynamo?

Already, I think, we have answered most of these questions. Not the South alone, but the whole modern world, after its recent bold escape from superstition, is in fact trembling before its own shadow. We are trying to run away from our shadows under the delusion that we are running away from the past. But it is as useless to run away from the past as it is to run away from what we call life. Wherever we go, we still carry life, and that root of life which is the past, in our tribal memories, in our nerves, in our arteries. All we can do is to deny or distort the shifting semblance we know as reality. And so the fantasy of abominations has stolen the proud stilts of the romantics. To borrow Gerald W. Johnson's amusing expression, Southern fiction 'comes stepping high,' as of old, only it is now stepping over a bog instead of a battlefield. Farther away, beyond the authentic masters of horror, press and push the rows of ambitious amateurs, who imagine that they are realists because they have tasted a stew of spoilt meat. But it takes more than spoilt meat to make realism. It takes, among other attributes, a seasoned philosophy and a mature outlook on life.

For thirty years I have had a part in the American literary scene, either as a laborer in the vineyard or as a raven croaking on a bust of Pallas. In all these years I have found that the only permanent law in art, as in the social order, is the law of change. Although it may be true that we cannot change human nature, history proves on every page, as John Chamberlain has reminded us, that we can and constantly do change human behavior. I have seen fashions in fiction and in behavior shift and alter and pass away while we watched them. I have seen reputations swell out and burst with wind and shrivel up into damp rags of India-rubber. I have seen, not without sardonic amusement, the balance of power in American letters pass from genteel mediocrity with hair on the face to truculent mediocrity with down on the chest.

For these and other reasons, the last position I would assume is that of the lone defender of the human species in modern fiction. I needed no peep at war to teach me that we live among evils. I needed no 'planned economy' to prove to me that these evils are of our own making. It may be true, as our more popular novelists assure us, that we are doomed. It may be true that all is lost to us but moral and physical disintegration, and we should hasten out, while it is yet day, to gather in that rich literary harvest. This, I repeat, may be true. One may point to life and prove anything; it all depends on the pointing. And despair itself may be vital; it may be strong; it may be courageous; though only worms can survive the damp chill of negation. Few things, however, are more certain than this: — the literature that crawls too long in the mire will lose at last the power of standing erect. On the farther side of deterioration lies the death of a culture.

But, even so, when the worst has been written, it is not an ignoble fate — it is not an unhappy fate — to go down still fighting against the inevitable. That is a triumph of the will, not a surrender; and if nothing pleasanter may be said of the inevitable, at least it is worth fighting. Whatever contemporary fiction may think of love, the world has shown from the beginning that it loves fighters. Nor is the impulse toward something better, or at least different, confined to humanity; it runs back and forth through all nature. We are too apt to forget that the earliest recorded conquest over destiny was achieved by a fish. Nowadays, while we puzzle over the human mass movement back into the slime, it is well to remind ourselves of our first revolutionary ancestor, that 'insane fish,' so lovingly commemorated by James Branch Cabell, 'who somehow evolved the idea that it was his duty to live on land, and eventually succeeded in doing it.' Surely that high exploit deserves a more appropriate memorial than sophisticated barbarism and the sentimental cult of corruption.

The revolutionary fish no longer leaps. Although the word Revolution is in the air, the true spirit is wanting. Instead, we breathe in a suffocating sense of futility. That liberal hope of which we dreamed in my youth appears to have won no finer freedom than an age of little fads and the right to cry ugly words in the street. Not for whims like these do men unite and live or die happily. The true revolution may end in a ditch or in the shambles; but it must begin in the stars. There must be bliss, as Wordsworth found, in that dawn, 'And human nature seeming born again.'

I am not asking the novelist of the Southern Gothic school to change his material. The Gothic as Gothic, not as pseudo-realism, has an important place in our fiction. Besides, I know too well that the born novelist does not choose his subject; he is chosen by it. All I ask him to do is to deal as honestly with living tissues as he now deals with decay, to remind himself that the colors of putrescence have no greater validity for our age, or for any age, than have — let us say, to be very daring — the cardinal virtues. For, as a great modern philosopher has written: 'An honorable end is the one thing that cannot be taken from a man.'

PETRARCH

Books come at my call and return when I desire them; they are never out of humor and they answer all my questions with readiness. Some present in review before me the events of past ages; others reveal to me the secrets of Nature. These teach me how to live, and those how to die; these dispel my melancholy by their mirth, and amuse me by their sallies of wit. Some there are who prepare my soul to suffer everything, to desire nothing, and to become thoroughly acquainted with itself. In a word they open the door to all the arts and sciences.

RAFAEL SABATINI, *citing the myths of William Tell and the Man in the Iron Mask, upholds avowed Fiction against alleged Fact.*

HISTORICAL FICTION

IT IS less of a truism than it seems, to say that the writer of historical fiction seeks his inspiration in history, for if he has a proper sense of his calling he will take for his foundations none of the legends disguised under that name.

Elsewhere in this connection — in the preface to my play 'The Tyrant' — I have enunciated a truth which it seems to me worth while to repeat and examine.

It runs as follows:

'It is demanded of the writer of fiction, whether novelist or dramatist, that the events he sets forth shall be endowed with the quality of verisimilitude. What he writes need not necessarily be true; but, at least, it must seem to be true, so that it may carry that conviction without which interest fails to be aroused. The historian appears to lie under no such restraining obligation. Whilst avowed Fiction is scornfully rejected when it transcends the bounds of human probability, alleged Fact would sometimes seem to be the more assured of enduring acceptance, the more flagrantly impossible and irreconcilable are its details.'

If this were not true it would have been impossible for the innumerable myths that cumber serious history to have found their way into it and to have become so firmly established that it is almost impossible to uproot them.

To illustrate the point it may not be amiss to consider in some details two such myths as those of William Tell and the Man in the Iron Mask.

For some centuries the figure of William Tell, that foremost of Swiss national heroes has been conspicuous in the Pantheon of history. To this day his image, shouldering a crossbow, is to be seen on the Swiss stamps.

There is practically no important fact of his life with which we are not acquainted. We learn that he was born and lived at Bürglen. A chapel dedicated to his memory, adorned with scenes from his heroic life, stands upon the site. It was built somewhere about 1580. Himself noble — his coat of arms was included by Zurlauben among those of the armigerous families of Uri — he was connected by marriage with the patrician house of Attinghausen.

He was farming his lands at Bürglen in the dawn of the fourteenth century, at the time when the nucleus of the Swiss Confederation was emerging from the Forest States about Lake Lucerne. Three of these states — Schwytz, Uri and Unterwalden — entered into a solemn league to defend these free communities from the encroachments of the predatory Hapsburgs. In this league William Tell is a prominent figure.

An Austrian Landvogt, or bailiff, named Gessler, presumably suspecting the existence of this anti-Hapsburg league, hit upon an ingenious device for discovering the malcontents. He caused a cap of maintenance to be set up on a pole in the market place at Altdorf, and demanded that all passers-by should do reverence to this emblem of Austrian sovereignty.

Tell comes along, accompanied by his little son. He pays no heed to the emblem. Challenged, he stoutly refuses to uncover. He is seized. Gessler supervenes. Out of a refinement of cruelty, aware of Tell's great reputation as a marksman, he gives him a chance of saving his forfeited life. If he can from a given distance hit an apple placed on the head of his son, he shall go free; but if he fails both he and his son shall perish.

Tell accepts the condition, having indeed little choice in the matter. His quarrel unerringly splits the apple, which must have brought disappointment to the tyrant who sat his horse, a witness of the feat. Gessler is reluctant to let him go. He questions him about a second quarrel, which Tell had taken from his quiver and bestowed ready to his hand in his belt. With the proud, reckless courage of the hero, Tell avows its purpose. If the first quarrel had missed the apple, the second one would certainly not have missed Gessler's heart.

Now that is not the way to speak to a man invested with despotic power. Gessler orders him to be bound, and brought along to the Castle of Küssnacht, where the bailiff resided, and where he proposes to give himself the pleasure of hanging this stubborn rogue.

They embark in Gessler's barge, so as to cross the lake to Küssnacht. A storm springs up. They are in great danger. Tell is a powerful fellow, a skilled waterman with experience of lake-storms. He is unbound and given the tiller. He brings the boat alongside of a rocky promontory. Then snatching up his cross-bow, which had been carelessly left within his reach, he leaps ashore, and in the very act spurns the boat back among the windswept waves.

On this rocky promontory, known as Tell's Platte, stands a commemorative chapel built at the end of the fifteenth or beginning of the sixteenth century.

He clambers up the mountain-side, whilst Gessler and his men are left to struggle with the storm. He makes his way to the heights above the Engegasse, the narrow way or hollow way, by Küssnacht, there to lie in wait for the homing Gessler; and there, eventually, he shoots him dead.

On this spot another commemorative chapel was built somewhere about 1570.

Tell's deed is the immediate cause of the rising of 1291 against the oppressors, in which Tell plays a leading part.

Again he is prominent in the Battle of Morgarten in 1315, which shattered the yoke which the Austrians sought to impose upon the Swiss.

Finally his death is placed in 1354. Heroic to the end, he loses his life in an attempt to save a child from drowning in the Schachenbach.

A statue of William Tell stands in the market-place at Altdorf, on the spot where he shot the apple from his son's head, erected there in 1895. There is another well-known statue of him in Lugano, and lesser statues are dotted up and down Switzerland in honour of this man who for centuries has been an inspiration in patriotism to the Swiss people.

To his skill with the cross-bow and his feat of marksmanship at Altdorf we may attribute the zeal with which the Swiss have aimed at rendering themselves a nation of marksmen. Periodically in Switzerland great shooting competitions — Schützenfeste, or shooting festivals — are held, attended by competitors from every country of Europe. And these undoubtedly rest upon the inspiration derived from the memory of William Tell, which, again, they serve to commemorate.

Now the story of Tell's adventures with Gessler presents many suspicious features; there is an opportuneness about the events, and a liberal seasoning of coincidence to help out dramatic situations. We are justified in suspecting that accretions have swollen the story. But it is staggering to find upon investigation that in spite of numerous statues erected to his memory, in spite of three chapels to commemorate his deeds, in spite of a coat of arms and a very circumstantial personal history, this man never lived at all. In short, that the whole story from beginning to end is a fabrication, a legend, a myth without the slightest foundation.

With the value of the legend as a national inspiration I am not concerned. My concern is solely with its right to a place in history. From this, at last, and very reluctantly, it has been expunged. Therefore I need not trouble now to trace its gradual growth and development through Johannes von Müller and Melchior Russ, back to the White Book of Sarnen in which it has its spurious source.

The Man in the Iron Mask and all the legends that have accumulated about him are much in the same case, for, properly speaking, there never was a Man in the Iron Mask. He is one of history's synthetic mysteries; by which I mean a mystery gradually built up by successive historical writers in their endeavours to explain the initial mystery discovered in the earliest accounts of his existence.

Let us strip away these speculative explanations, which have been accumulating for two hundred and fifty years — for the subject appears to be one of perennial fascination — and consider the few bare bones of fact with which we are left.

In the reign of Louis XIV there was in the frontier fortress of Pignerol in 1679 a prisoner whose head and face were covered by a mask.

After a time, when Pignerol — the modern Pinerolo — was given up to Savoy (in 1694) this prisoner was removed thence with others and transferred to the Ile Sainte Marguérite. Four years later, in 1698, he was transferred again, this time to the Bastille, where he died in 1703. In the Register of the Bastille his name was given as Marchioly, and his age at the time of his death was stated to have been about forty-five.

The mask covering his head and face lend him at the outset a mysteriousness which is an incitement to invention. Since the mask is the starting-point of the mystery, it should also be the starting-point of investigation.

Our first shattering discovery is that the mask is made of velvet — a sort of casque, or helmet, covering the entire head, fitting tightly to it and held in position by steel springs on each side.

It is not difficult to perceive how fancy was captured by those steel springs. Attention becomes so absorbed in them that soon it loses sight of the fabric of the mask itself. As we advance, narratives cease to mention it. They mention merely a mask with steel springs. Steel and iron are, after all, akin; and perhaps because iron has a slightly more sinister connotation — I can think of no other reason — it comes to be preferred by the sensation-monger. Presently the actual springs go the way of the velvet; only the metallic substance remains; the manufacture of the iron mask is complete. The mystery has become deeper and more sinister in consequence. Therefore, speculation must exert itself still more actively to explain it. Such a mask must naturally be fixed and immovable. Why else should it be made of iron? Eighteenth-century writers are busy clamping, rivetting, or padlocking this iron pot onto the prisoner's head. Inconveniences arising from the inability to wash and the growth of hair and beard are not considered.

A reason for this mask must be provided, and imagination goes briskly to provide it. If we are at such pains to conceal the features of a man, it follows that the disclosure of his identity must be attended by the gravest consequences. It also follows that his features are well known, that he is a person of some worldly consequence. Therefore it comes to be reported that he is treated with the utmost deference, and that he is always addressed as 'Monseigneur.'

I pass over such stories as that of the message scratched on a metal dish, which he flung through the window to be picked up by a poor fisherman, who escaped being put to death, so as to bury the terrible secret, only because he was unable to read.

We are told, by way of stressing his consequence, that he has a governor in the person of Monsieur de Saint-Mars, who moves with him from prison to prison. Here cause and effect have been confused. Saint-Mars was governor of Pignerol when the man was first imprisoned there. Later Saint-Mars was transferred to the governorship of Sainte-Marguérite. Later still, when Pignerol was ceded to Savoy, some of the prisoners, among whom was the man in the mask, were conveyed to Sainte-Marguérite. Finally, when Saint-Mars was made governor of the Bastille he certainly did take this prisoner with him. But it was the prisoner who accompanied Saint-Mars, not Saint-Mars the prisoner, as we are asked to believe.

The title of 'Monseigneur,' by which we are told that he was addressed, materially narrows the field of conjecture upon his identity. When the most searching investigation fails to discover the disappearance in Europe of any personage of the eminence implied by this title, you would suppose that speculation would confess itself at fault and would turn in its tracks. Not at all. That is not the way of sensation-mongers. Since no living Monseigneur can be discovered to have disappeared, the identity of the prisoner is sought among the dead ones. One man after another of monseigneurial rank is put forward as having survived a falsely reported death.

This mask is said to conceal the features of the Duke of Monmouth, beheaded in 1685; of the Duke of Beaufort, who died in Candia in 1669; of Louis Comte de Vermandois, the son of Louis XIV by Louise de la Vallière, who died in 1683; of Fouquet, who had certainly been imprisoned in Pignerol, and who died there in 1680, and of several others, amongst whom we find the son of Oliver Cromwell.

Voltaire is responsible for so much of this fury of speculation and so much of this nonsense that it is scarcely too much to say that he is the inventor of the Man in the Iron Mask. It is he, in his 'Siècle de Louis XIV,' who to explain the masked prisoner of Pignerol, imagines an elder brother of Louis XIV of a countenance so strongly resembling the king's that, in putting him away, so as to avoid political complications, it was necessary to cover his features lest they should of themselves betray this terrible secret. Because there is something lacking here to make this story quite convincing, another pen, a little later, explains that this elder brother is really only a half-brother, a bastard brother, the child of Anne of Austria and Cardinal Mazarin.

In the second half of the eighteenth century, a work appeared in France under the title of 'The Mémoirs of the Duc de Richelieu.' It seems to have been taken seriously until it was discovered that in reality it was an historical novel from the pen of the Abbé Soulavie. From this we learn that the secret of the Man in the Iron Mask was disclosed by the Regent d'Orléans to one of his mistresses, who, in her turn, disclosed it to the Duc de Richelieu. To stress the terrible nature of this secret the main facts are actually printed in cipher. But in a cipher so puerile that the dullest may decipher it almost at sight.

In this version, the author, with the laudable object of giving the story a twist less damaging to the honour of a chaste and virtuous queen, presents the Man in the Mask as the twin brother of Louis XIV: the second born, and therefore the elder, as being the first conceived — a point for which there is neither biological nor legal sanction.

Those who are familiar with Dumas will remember what excellent use he makes of this extremely romantic material in his 'Vicomte de Bragelonne.' In some ways this fantastic story is the most plausible that has been put forward to fit the accretions accumulated about the bare facts of the Man in the Iron Mask.

In 1801 a story was current that this scion of the royal house of France had left a son who had settled in Corsica under the assumed but suggestive name of Da Buona Parte (i.e., 'of good stock'). Here it is no longer the hand of the sensation-monger that is at work, but that of the propagandist of whom it is also necessary to beware when reading history.

To leave these fictions and return for a moment to the known facts, Marchioly, the name in the Register of the Bastille, appears to be a corruption of the Italian name Mattioli.

A man named Ercole Mattioli, born in Bologna in 1640, was minister to the Duke of Mantua, and governor of Casale. This frontier fortress was coveted by Louis XIV, and Mattioli sold it to him for one hundred thousand crowns. But on the eve of its occupation by the French, Mattioli double-crossed the King by betraying the transaction. Louis XIV was not the man to allow this to go unpunished. But he was faced with obvious difficulties in punishing a foreign subject. However, in 1679 his agents kidnapped Mattioli, and he disappears.

Now 1679 is the year of the arrival at Pignerol of the prisoner in the mask, subsequently registered at the Bastille as Marchioly.

Need we look further? Would anyone have looked further but for the mask and the irresponsible transmutation of its substance?

The mask itself remains to be explained. It is possible that, considering the violation of a frontier entailed by the nature of the arrest, it may have been expedient to impose it upon a prisoner whose anonymity it was desired to ensure. On the other hand, it is just as possible that the prisoner was masked of his own volition. After all, the wearing of masks by state prisoners is by no means uncommon in the seventeenth century, when the mask was recognised as a more or less ordinary article of apparel. Certain it is that the type of mask worn by the prisoner of Pignerol was one which he could put on and off at will, and that it was for this very purpose that it was equipped with the steel springs which are responsible for the vast literature of the subject, amounting by now to some fifty volumes. When we reflect that, before the discovery and manufacture of rubber, steel springs were the only elastic substance known to man, the purpose of these becomes manifest and all mystery vanishes.

The innumerable narratives as fantastic and groundless as those two we have examined would never have found their abiding place in history if historical writers, instead of hammering them in by careless reiteration, had applied to them the tests which common-sense dictates should be applied to statements relating to present-day events. In adopting these statements responsible writers proceed cautiously. For one thing, there is today a law of libel to inspire this caution. It helps us to remember that all human evidence is liable to error, as a result of faulty observation or faulty interpretation of the facts observed. It is also liable to deliberate dishonesty, the calculated deception practised from motives of prejudice, or bigotry, for purposes of political propaganda, of personal profit, or merely out of a morbid passion for the sensational and the defamatory.

Human nature does not change. As it is today, so has it been in the past. Therefore it is the duty of the historian to deal with the evidence supplied by witnesses or chroniclers of the events in precisely the same manner as obtains in civilized courts today.

Let me illustrate the point by briefly considering the evidence of the incest of which history accuses some, if not all, of the members of the House of Borgia. It is the basis of a great deal of question-begging in that history and helps to render credible by its undeniable turpitude the other fantastic turpitudes laid to that family's charge.

The accusation, we find, is first uttered by Giovanni Sforza of Pesaro, Lucrezia Borgia's first husband; and just as he supplies the source of it, so he remains the only witness of any authority, since, from his relationship with the family, he must be accepted as possessing that intimate knowledge which certainly could not be claimed by any other of the contemporary scandal-mongers who repeated it.

Since, properly speaking, there is no competent corroboration of this hideous charge, it becomes doubly necessary to investigate, as a test of credibility, the character and possible motives of our single witness.

What actually did he say, and in what circumstances did he say it?

Giovanni Sforza's marriage was annulled on the grounds of his incapacity to consummate it. This he, himself, ended by admitting over his signature. Before admitting it, however, and possibly stung by the ridicule into which it brought him, he alleged that he had been coerced into consenting to the divorce, that the grounds urged for it were false, and that Lucrezia had been taken away from him by her father, who wanted her for himself — '*per usare con lei*,' in his own actual words.

Malice may reasonably be suspected here, urging us to look closely into the attendant facts for matter that will either confirm or refute the accusation. To confirm it nothing is discoverable. To refute it we find the following considerations:

1. If Giovanni Sforza knew of these incestuous relations between his wife and her father, how came he to tolerate them, and why did he wait until the promotion of the divorce to make his denunciation?
2. That her father 'wanted her for himself' is not supported by the sequel. For nine months later we find her being given in marriage to Alfonso of Aragon, the nephew of the King of Naples.
3. It is not conceivable that the royal House of Naples and the sovereign Ferrara House of Este (in which Lucrezia found her third husband) would have accepted a woman stained by such practices. From this we may infer that the charge of incest was regarded by her contemporaries, who were competent to judge, as the groundless and vindictive utterance of reckless spite.

So as to test the truth of the statements upon which history depends, the first inquiry should concern the qualifications of the witness testifying; it should seek to discover what facilities he enjoyed for observing the matters which he reports. In the second place, it should be investigated whether motives of interest or bias might sway him in one direction or another; and, in the third place, corroboration of his statements is to be sought from other witnesses and from what we may term the logic of the actual events.

Only by such processes of sifting and collating can the truth of any past transaction ever be reached. It is certainly true that in the main these processes have been scrupulously followed by conscientious and painstaking historical writers. But it is no less true that very often they have not. There is an easy road to popularity by pandering to the love of the sensational, the bizarre or the macabre, and this road has been diligently pursued by many of those who supply the sources of history and by still more of those who compile from them.

The foolish prig who conceives that he is impressive when he asserts that he never reads fiction because he is a student of fact, and who rejects with disdain the well-made, careful, and instructive historical novel, will consume with proud delight (because it gives him, at the cost of very little effort, the sense of being a student) the ill-made, grotesque, impossible, and sordid fictions artlessly presented under the spurious label of Fact. It was probably one of these who, as a result of the particular well from which he drew his bucket, first asserted that Truth is stranger than Fiction; but he failed to discover that well-made fiction is never stranger than fact.

It is the function of art to hold the mirror up to nature. Applied to the art of fiction, this means that it should hold the mirror up to fact. And this is as true of historical fiction as of fiction dealing with contemporary life.

It is idle to suppose that even indifferent historical fiction can be written without a deal of research and a close and intimate study, not only of the major events, but of the manners, the customs, the minutiae of daily life obtaining in the epoch chosen and exerting their influence upon the characters that moved in it.

Just as the novel dealing with contemporary life should be an illustration and elucidation of the present, so should the historical novel be an illustration and elucidation of the period selected from the past. If it accomplishes this, then it is not too much to say that it will supply, in addition to entertainment, more valuable instruction than any of the histories in which events have been falsified and historical characters have been distorted.

A period novel need not concern itself entirely with historical characters and historical happenings. It may do so, of course. On the other hand, it may do no more than present an invented story developed by means of imaginary characters, but set against a real background to which story and characters must bear some real and true relationship. Or it may lie somewhere between these two varieties, blending events that are real with events that are reasonably and logically imagined, and characters that lived with characters that the author has invented.

In presenting characters that have lived, the conscientious novelist will strive to draw portraits that are as true to the originals as it lies within his power to make them.

If I seek in my own work the illustrations I need of the main classes into which I have subdivided the historical novel, it is solely because naturally I am better acquainted with — and it is easier for me to dissect — my own work than that of others.

As an example of a novel of the first type I mention, I may put forward 'The King's Minion.' For this I did not invent a story. I scarcely invented even a minor character. I took from history an episode that appeared to me in itself to be intensely dramatic, and sought to the best of my ability to give it actuality, to set the characters through which it was developed, moving and breathing as in life. I permitted myself, however, to imagine a solution to the mystery presented by the murder of Sir Thomas Overbury. But even here my imagination was ridden on a tight rein, and it is my settled persuasion that the explanation I supply is the correct one. All that I permitted myself to imagine was imagined as the result of close study and close reasoning. I cannot prove that there were two simultaneous conspiracies to murder Overbury which became entangled — this supplying the pivot of my own plot — but I can and do assert that all the evidence points strongly in that direction when considered in the light of the well-known treacherous characteristics of James I. So that my 'The King's Minion,' whilst remaining an historical novel, offers at the same time an historical study of certain important happenings in the reign of the first Stuart King of England, and is not concerned with anything outside of these.

'Scaramouche' will serve for an example of a novel in my second class. Here we have an invented character moving through an invented personal history. But he is — as every character of a novel in this class must be — one of the natural offspring of the circumstances and habits of mind of the time into which he is born. His character is moulded by these; his fortunes (however fictitious) are shaped by them. The background against which he moves and into which he merges is borrowed from history; and to this extent we have here again an historical study of an epoch, although it is subservient to the fictitious history of Scaramouche himself.

'Captain Blood' lies between the two. Although not actually a real character, his attributes and a great many of the vicissitudes through which he passes have been lifted from the lives of men who actually lived.

The early part of his story is really the story of Henry Pitman. A surgeon who had been a considerable traveller on the Continent of Europe, Pitman came home, to the West of England, at about the time of the Monmouth Rebellion. Persuaded to give his skill and his labour to mitigate the sufferings of some wounded followers of Monmouth, he was arrested for this, tried before Jeffreys at the Bloody Assize, sentenced to death with a batch of others, the sentence being subsequently commuted to transportation to the overseas plantations. Shipped to Barbados and sold there as a slave, the fact of his being a surgeon served to ease his lot. Skilled men of medicine were scarce in the Colonies, and his purchaser found it not only desirable but profitable to set him to practise his profession rather than to labour with the other slaves in the plantations. Hence Pitman enjoyed a certain amount of freedom, and he used it to plan an escape, associating with himself in this a group of rebels-convict who had been shipped out with him into slavery.

It will be seen by those who have read 'Captain Blood' that up to this point his story runs closely parallel with that of Pitman in general outline. In detail it follows it with the same closeness, but incorporating matter from other sources, so as to complete the picture of social history in England and in Barbados in the latter half of the seventeenth century.

Blood's story ceases to be based on Pitman's from the moment of the escape. For my protagonist in what is really the second part of the novel, dealing with Blood's career as a buccaneer, I employ several models, of whom Sir Henry Morgan is one, and I derive from the buccaneer history of that eye-witness Esquemeling the foundation of fact for the events which I invent or adapt to my own purposes.

There is, I should imagine, no fundamental difference between my own methods and those of any other writer of historical fiction. And when all is said, these methods are not very different from those of the writer upon contemporary themes. Each must inform himself as closely and accurately as possible of the realities of the life with which he deals.

The aim of all fiction being to present a story that shall be to fact as weft to warp, I can conceive of no reason why a transaction invented to fit the days of, say, Queen Elizabeth should be of less merit, interest, or appeal than a transaction invented to fit the days of President Roosevelt.

The writing of historical romance certainly makes heavy demands upon an author. Before he can come to it, he must have rendered himself by study and research so familiar with every phase and detail of the life of the period chosen that he can move at ease within it, and produce his effects so that his narrative, without being clogged by a parade of the knowledge he will have assimilated, will yet be fully informed and enlivened by it.

That, at least, is the ambitious aim; and if we are fortunate as well as diligent, we sometimes achieve it.

RALPH WALDO EMERSON

The permanence of all books is fixed by no effort friendly or hostile, but by their own specific gravity or the intrinsic importance of their contents to the constant mind of man.

HENRY JAMES

The deepest quality of any work of art will always be the quality of the mind of its producer.

HENRY SEIDEL CANBY

Style is like happiness. Everyone recognizes it, everyone describes it, but no two people agree as to its exact nature.

GERTRUDE ATHERTON

What is a husband to a book?

VOLTAIRE

If I had a son who wanted to write, I should wring his neck, out of sheer paternal affection.

ISABEL PATERSON

Authors should never be seen. Their place is in the home. They are no great treat there either, but the family has to put up with them. Whatever they have to give us is in their work.

GERTRUDE ATHERTON
curses the commonplace, and recommends to all writers a thorough course in endocrinology.

WANTED: IMAGINATION

I

HOW many different kinds of novels there are! Historical novels, past and present, novels concentrated on men and women of high breeding and inherited position, on the small town, the middle-class, the proletariat; on current economic developments as they affect the individual or group; the regional novel with or without a universal application; that lucrative variety that can only be characterized as Mush for Morons; the calorific, so popular with the inquisitive young, and drab women; the detective-mystery-crime story beloved of all grades from master to butler, from professor to freshman. Well has it been said: there is no Public, there are publics. All these contrastive types of fiction find, in varying degrees, a place, and a band of followers. Judging by occasional supersales, certain novels please all the publics; which merely proves that the general public is subject at times to one more mass impulse, or that intelligent persons like variety.

Many of these so-called novels should not come under that

head at all. They are merely long stories. Although I am, off and on, a mystery fan, I should never quarrel with any stern critic who relegated that offshot to the Yarn Class. And the same may be said of the story of adventure, and that order of historical fiction that deals not with the psychology of great personalities — if they are introduced at all — but with their glittering shells and the sensational events of which they were the protagonists. Mere length does not make a novel.

What then is a novel? The question is apt to jar a hornet's nest into action, for many critics resent too strict a classification of anything. Well, I dislike anything that savors of the hidebound myself, and will forbear to maintain that a novel *must* have a theme, although there is no question that a theme centralizes a novel and adds to its dignity and importance. Let that pass. Some very readable and even distinguished novels merely meander along, all the interest centered in one or two characters; psychology and style so admirable that one asks for nothing more.

Nevertheless, I do maintain that a novel to merit its classification must have at least two things: it must be written on the *plan of life*, and its characters must be so powerfully realized and presented that they dissever themselves from the page — as living realities as any of our acquaintances in the flesh; not mere types that never get their heads above the printed line. Whether our author has a theme or not, when he finally hurls himself at his desk with a muttered 'Today I begin this damn thing or perish in the attempt,' he must have two things in mind: his principal character and his *mis-en-scène*. He knows perfectly well whether he is going to set his stage in New York or Timbuctû, and some very real person has been prowling about his fiction tract demanding to be let out. Perhaps he even has a fairly concrete idea of his first chapter. Perhaps he merely plunges in, trusting to that rotten spot in his brain, grandly called the Creative Faculty, to spring to action. In either case he may toil and moil over that first chapter, rewriting it half a dozen times, until he works up his mental muscle and gets fairly started. Then if he is a novelist and not a yarn spinner (note that I do not say *mere* yarn spinner; I have a grateful affection for that lively stepchild of the Art of Fiction), he then lets his chronicle write itself, restrained only by his guiding hand. Imagination is the one divine gift granted to mortals, but to let it dart too far ahead of reason would be as disastrous as if an impeccable automobile were raced over a cliff by an accomplished driver intoxicated with speed.

Out of the characters, finally probed to the writer's satisfaction, grow the incidents that reveal them to themselves and to the public; these incidents in turn react upon the characters, sometimes with minor, sometimes with startling results, but always carrying both characters and story a step, or a leap, forward. This, in plain language, is development by action, even if the action be skull-bound and has nothing in common with visible causations. This process goes on until it is time to have mercy on the reader and stop. For such is the plan of life, and a novel is something else unless it faithfully follows that plan. What we do tomorrow or a year hence is the result of what we do today, even making allowance for accident or disease. And all is the result of character working hand-in-hand, however unaware, with the immutable law of cause and effect.

Even within these seemingly rigid lines the author has ample opportunity for drama both mental and extraneous. But it must be inevitable. If dragged in arbitrarily, then is he second-rate. In every performance of their lives those characters act as they alone, not as someone else, would act in similar conditions; the products, they, of heredity, early regional fate, family influences, too much affection or too little — all the forces that swirl about childhood, and so often make life a hard battle for those who, ill-equipped, try, so far as is possible, to make themselves over. To grapple with life and conquer it requires qualities of mind and character which, given intelligence, they observe in the fortunate, but lack in themselves. This, by the way, would be a fair sample of a thematic novel.

To use a crude illustration of logical sequence, take the hero of a novel who inadvertently runs down and kills a man while speeding. Is he a hit-and-runner, or does he pull up, turn back, and carry his victim to a hospital or morgue regardless of his own possible fate? If the author makes him do the wrong thing for the sake of drama, or to give an exhibition of conscience-psychology later on, then again is he second-rate. Some men are incapable of panic, just as some men are incapable of sneaking out of any tight place.

And yet in what a dilemma may the author find himself if the man he has conscientiously unfolded finds himself sent to State's Prison for manslaughter. It has been impossible to prevent the imagination from darting ahead and gaining a fair idea at least of how that man will run his span; by the middle of the book the author knows him pretty intimately and his general conditions as well. If economic disaster is to overwhelm him, in common with millions of others, his creator can safely predict how he will meet it, although he refuses to consider details until they arise. And then, presto! this man is in prison for a term of years, the natural course of his life interrupted, his character, his disposition, his very ego, subject to ineluctable changes. What in heaven's name, cries the distracted author, will he be when he comes out? And how am I to know, unless I get sent up myself, exactly what happens to his soul day by day, year by year? What embitters him, ennobles him, turns him into a cynic, an uplifter, a brooder, a Pollyanna.... Oh, horror! Psychologists tell us that every man is a potential criminal. Are not children natural-born thieves? Suppose he emerges a gangster! Well as I thought I knew him I never counted on this. And what is worse, those who know nothing of the dire problems of authorship will denounce me as whimsical, capricious, deliberately going off at a tangent for the sake of sensationalism.

What shall our haggard author do? Go back over those chapters of meticulous progression, and try to eliminate the minute invisible steps which led up to that accident? Can he, can he, and retain his intellectual integrity? Well, that is his job. We leave him to his fate.

I think it was Taine, possibly in his 'Littérature Anglaise,' who advised creative authors to lift some type of man out of the commonplace conditions to which he was apparently doomed for the rest of his life and transfer him to an environment, replete with change and opportunity, where he could develop his latent potentialities. Many a clerk, for instance, dimly conscious of a streak of originality, but harnessed by circumstance, might thus be given the chance to become a hero, a great leader, a prophet, or a criminal. If Fate has been unkind to him, here is an opportunity for the amiable author to come to the rescue. And a fascinating game for the author.

This country is full of fine upstanding young Americans, well-enough-born, well-brought-up, 'straight' both by instinct and training, vaguely idealistic, as youth so often is, who have worked their way through college or been sent there by parents at a considerable sacrifice; then, after some difficulty, 'land a job,' and give to it their best efforts, not only because it is the right thing to do, but in the hope of one day 'rising to the top.' They are sailing along smoothly, content enough save for the natural impatience of youth, when suddenly their country is plunged into war. Fired by the slogan 'Your country needs you,' they enlist. Of war they know nothing save that it is a great adventure, and was the most interesting part of their history books.

Suppose our author takes six of these young men, fine average specimens, and puts them through two years of war's abnormalities: two years of life in filthy trenches, with rats running over their faces at night, the companionship of low-bred men unspeakably vulgar, the roaring hell of battle succeeded by weeks, possibly months, of monotony, during which they learn to long for that brief respite back of the lines where there is liquor and women and oblivion; where they learn to curse the old men who send the young out to be slaughtered, or contract disease, and to part with the last of their illusions.

Someone has said that a man brings out of the great trials of life what he takes into them, but that is only a half-truth, as M. Taine, who recognized the latent possibilities in every man, could have told him. Most of the plays and novels that have used the World War as a theme have delighted in characters turned into brutes, weaklings, or vulgarians whose vocabulary is hair-raising: the dire result of life in the trenches, in shell holes, behind the lines. It would be interesting if some author with more imagination would take the six young Americans I have indicated and lead a few of them forth, if not exactly ennobled by the experience, at least not hopelessly demoralized. Personally I have met quite a number of men who have been through several wars and they seemed to me very decent citizens.

II

To return to our logically developed heroes in normal life. How sure we are at times that one of them longs to beat his wife, but literally cannot, so strong are his inhibitions! Not that men of the highest civilization do not now and again even murder their wives, or someone else, but even so that dark streak in their egos has always been there, however submerged, and the author, now and then gives his reader a flashing glimpse into those haunted depths as he drives his victim of 'inherited factors,' circumstance, early inimical forces, along his destined path. The accomplished author knows how to make inconsistencies consistent.

As to murder. Many a time have I wanted to commit murder, and not infrequently on some character in a book who so roused my fury that if I had a weak heart or high blood pressure I should have succumbed long ago. These murderous impulses are healthy, and the inhibitions planted during our plastic years keep us within the law. That is, if we are the fortunate ones. Born in a lower stratum, with drunken or stupid parents and that black streak, inherited like as not from piratical ancestors, then might we make an undignified exit at the end of a rope or an electric current. Are we then mere victims of fate, our lives and ends predestined? Pity the poor character in search of an author. Once he is in those inexorable hands he might as well try to wriggle out of the coils of a boa constrictor who has taken a fancy to him as he gathered orchids in a South American forest. Sad to reflect upon. But anyone who has tried, say, to remake the ego of a girl of sixteen will know what I mean.

On the other hand (returning to our soldier boys), many a

man who has secretly believed himself to be a physical coward will go over the top full of wild courage owing to the sudden response of his adrenal glands; his comrade, perhaps, advancing into that fiery deluge by sheer will-power, pride, breeding, patriotic resignation, with no furious hormones in his blood stream to aid him in that supreme ordeal. All these things have to be taken into consideration by our novelist. If he simply cannot permit a timid but beloved character to act the coward when death beckons, then must he make him a present of sound but dormant adrenals, and, with a light touch, give a hint now and again of their presence before that awful moment when kindly nature comes to the rescue. In fact, if every author of history, biography, and fiction would take a course in endocrinology he would make fewer mistakes. Glands go to the very root of character.

III

This is all very well, but goes so far and no farther to make a novel interesting, and if a work of fiction is not interesting, no matter how carefully considered, it might better not be written at all. The trouble with most of our regional novels, for instance, many of them 'worthy' enough to win the Pulitzer Prize, is that they are too much in one key, both characters and events too uniformly unexciting, the tempo too slow, the author too intent upon good reporting instead of producing a work of art. The same may be said of the proletarian novel, whose perpetrators are so painfully serious, so contemptuous of art or even of craftsmanship, that the reader yawns and wonders why they adopted the fiction form; articles on the same subject in newspapers and magazines being more impressive and interesting. The novel with a purpose is a deadly thing unless handled by a genius, and genuises are as rare as cold nights in the tropics. Still, these regional novels, at least, have won a public, so why cavil?

Here is a word of advice to the young novelist intent upon reforming the world, exposing this system or that, exalting the proletariat and wishful of sending all capitalists to the stake. *Study craftsmanship.* Nature may have denied you genius or even talent, everything but a terrific earnestness and a certain facility of expression. But craftsmanship you may achieve if you condescend to give your mind to it, and win you a public beyond the narrow confines of near-intellectuals. Art may be forever beyond you, and magic a word to be regarded with contempt and suspicion, but craftsmanship brought to a state of canny perfection may compel the reader to go on provided he can be induced to begin. You could have no better model than Galsworthy. After his first few novels he gradually descended into the light fiction class and became so trivial and repetitive that a week after finishing one of those stories it was hard to distinguish it in memory from any that had preceded it. It is true that he never lost his facility, polished style, commendable refinement. But these were not the qualities that enabled him to retain his public long after what imagination he originally possessed had expired. It was his truly magnificent craftsmanship. Many like myself must have vowed they would never waste time on another Galsworthy novel, but let any of us pick up one, idly intending to pass the time with a chapter or two of pleasant prose, and we were caught, netted, enticed. So closely interwoven, phrase by phrase, paragraph by paragraph, chapter by chapter, are those otherwise negligible works of fiction, that the reader can only compare himself to a fly gently enmeshed in the web of a beneficent spider, pleasantly sprayed with a mild anaesthetic. Craftsmanship. Technique. Many an author have they saved from an untimely end.

This new batch of writers, sponsored by the Little Magazines, who despise anything so canonical, will have their little day, perhaps, because critics and certain publics are mortally afraid of being condemned as out of date unless they hitch their wagon to the newest twinkler ballyhooed into fashion. But they can hope for nothing more. In a fairly long career I have seen innumerable literary fads flare up, bedazzle, cause any amount of excited chatter, flicker out. There are certain fundamentals that never will be ignored by the authentically gifted as long as Fiction retains its place among the arts. Holding fast to those, true originality never finds itself hampered. Sophocles in his day was severely criticized for taking liberties with certain minor conventions, Euripides for being too modern — or whatever the Greeks called it: when Catullus came along, the Latins had a word for it — neoteric. But all have survived, down through the centuries, because their feet were firmly planted the while they played ball with the stars. And each led his art one step farther along the road of progress. In all fairness it must be added that even the twinklers who appear now and again only to vanish into space because they lack the ingredients that go to the making of fixed stars, even they often leave a precipitation that, however minutely, enriches and expands the art of Fiction.

Returning to the first paragraph of this chapter: what then makes a novel interesting if art, technique, logic in the development of character, will not in themselves turn the trick? Aha! There is the crux of the whole matter, and the answer is almost too obvious to mention. Imagination. Genius. Talent. And whence come they? Recombination of brain cells down through the ages, perhaps. A dislocation of particles in that delicate organ due to pre-natal confusion. The brain is still as mysterious as life itself. Many have become writers of fiction by main strength, relying upon theses of immediate — or perennial — interest to compel the attention of the Public, but they are not the ones that survive. Fiction is the offspring of imagination, and if it doesn't live and glow as the facts of life pass through that crucible, then it has no place within the confines of Art. Fictionized facts and facts glorified by the light of Imagination are not always differentiated by the critics. It often takes Father Time to shove the one into a niche and the other into the ultimate bonfire.

It is a curious fact that many authors highly accomplished and with an indisputable talent for the story are oddly lacking in two things: the subtle gift of magic and the inherent power to 'hold up' a novel throughout several hundred pages. I believe that neither can be acquired. Magic is an endowment of nature like that personal magnetism that goes far deeper than charm and fascination, both of which may be acquired but are never potent if nature has been reluctant. Henry James had magic, and it was never more commanding than in his last and greatest novels when he seemed to take delight in making his devoted readers work as hard as if they were trying to solve a problem in Euclid. Louis Bromfield had it in a remarkable degree during his first phase; combined with certain peculiarities of form and an abundant and original imagination, it made him, to me at least, the most interesting of all the younger American writers. I wish he would hasten to recapture it. Phyllis Bottome is another of the fortunate who possesses this rare gift, oddly combined with a cool crystalline prose and a deadly logic in the development of character.

As to 'holding up.' Many novelists go along with a rush for a time, then seem to fall into holes. Sometimes they climb out, resume their original pace and come in strong on the home stretch. Others move with swift sure strokes until the last third or so when they begin to sag in interest, although no fault may be found with either prose or characterization. I fancy this is due to a lack of physical vitality; the long stretch is too much for their imaginative endurance, just as a runner may overestimate the strength of his legs. The fame of these writers rests on their short novels, and their popularity might have endured if they had condensed their more ambitious efforts. Of course even the greatest novelists have their dry pages, but that is due not so much to lack of vitality as to a deficiency in tact. They have fallen in love with detail and the reader may take it or leave it. Arnold Bennett must have maddened his readers at times, but personally I never cared what he wrote if only he would write it. He too was a magician.

IV

The author who finds that his especial gift is for the historical novel is confronted with a somewhat different problem from that of the contemporaneous novelist whose step-by-step evolution method I have described. After months of research work there is little he does not know about the lives of the characters he means to resurrect for the benefit of posterity (and his own pleasure). Above all he knows exactly how they died and when. No secret excitement in wondering and guessing, as with those characters typical of his own time, no matter how individual. But if anyone thinks that writing an historical novel is an easier job than the contemporary, let him try it. The historians he must wade through are, as a rule, purely objective in their treatment, recording only the major events in the lives of men long dead; a few may be admirable psychologists, but even they rarely give more than a glimpse of the inner man, almost never any details of his private life. After one has read perhaps two hundred books — history, memoirs, biographies, 'Life in the Times of...' etc. — in order to become as familiar with the background, environment, contemporaries, of the characters he has selected for renaissance as he is with his own, he has burrowed pretty deeply into their egos and is ready to undertake the task of reclothing their bones — or ashes — with plausible flesh and rescue them from the dark crypts of the past.

And as these personalities come alive in his fiction tract, his imagination, inspired by known facts, must supply all those minor events that link together the great recorded moments, and it is here that logical sequence comes in exactly as if he were writing a novel of his own times. He must find them and dramatize them; he must know how his people felt as well as acted, how they felt when they carefully refrained from acting, in other words, from giving themselves away. In short, the resurrection of the dead is no joke.

All this presupposes imagination on the part of the historical novelist, and, if he lacks this gift, far better he cultivate the regional or factual novel, which requires considerable invention but little imagination.

It is a curious fact that imagination has rarely been extolled by American critics, even by the stuffy old pundits who preceded that High Priest of the Commonplace, William Dean Howells. With neither imagination nor charm, originality nor distinction, but endowed with a mild gift for the story, indisputable sincerity, a profound belief that all human beings were as ordinary and middle-class as himself, Howells appeared at a moment when Fate was in an ironic mood. She took him firmly by the hand, led him to the top, bade the world accept him as 'The Master,' the Leading American Author. The majority of young writers slaved in his footsteps; to be a member of the Howells School, especially if acclaimed by The Master, brought them into instant notice, whether they could hold the position or not. Originality was out. Imagination something to be sneered at. Woe to the young author who had both and defied the prevailing fashion. Howells was my abomination; he was a blight from which American literature has never recovered. It was about 1910 that Clifford Smyth interviewed me for the *New York Times* and I delivered myself of my opinion of Howells, his fatal influence, and the excruciating boredom of his novels in no measured terms. I was living in Europe for the most part at that time and never had the faintest suspicion that my diatribe had attracted even passing attention until August, 1934, when I read an article on Howells in *The Saturday Review of Literature* by Mr. Bernard Smith which contained this astonishing statement: 'For a while — indeed for many years after Gertrude Atherton's energetic attack upon him, early in the century — it looked as though his stature would decline to the point of invisibility.' Well, I am glad of it. I only wish I had been old enough and bold enough to extinguish him before he got in his deadly work. He was a curse.

Even today, when American literature has to some extent, or rather in some quarters, shaken off his influence, the critics — and the younger men as well as the old fogies — either do not recognize imagination when they see it or it makes them uneasy; they fear to exalt what so few writers could live up to, and would relegate their favorites to a second place. They even go so far as to call historical novels — which, if first-class, demand imagination of a high order — 'the literature of escape.' Well, they generally run away from it themselves.

I have not the least intention of depreciating the novel of current life. Not only would Fiction drop of its own weight into a bottomless limbo if devoted exclusively to the historic past, but, quite aside from the fact that many of the greatest novels in all literature deal exclusively with the period in which they were written, it is a fact that serious novelists in general are writing *current history*, and their work will be as valuable for future reference as the more labored efforts of the historian *per se*. If a first-rate novelist's vogue passes, it is, more often than not, because he (or she) has devoted himself too exclusively to one phase of life only — the world of wealth and fashion, for instance — and the public has wearied of it; partly because it holds so little variety, and every intelligent reader likes change; but principally because so many other fields have been opened up in which the fictitious characters more closely resemble the average man and woman. This is particularly the case since the public has been thinking more about hanging on to what little it has than aspiring to the glittering 'Horseshoe' in the 'Met.' The great middle class and the lower middle class, in their Twentieth-Century developments, offer a fertile field to the novelist and have found admirable if not very exciting chroniclers. The trouble also with the older generation of novelists is that they remain immobile both as regards conditions and vocabulary. They approve neither of new words nor of modern divagations, and in consequence, are 'dated.' Booth Tarkington is a notable exception. He set a standard for himself in the days of his youth and has never fallen below it, but at the same time he has kept in the very middle of Life's swiftly moving stream and escaped being marooned in a backwater.

A further word about standards. How bewildered a young writer must be when he reads six different reviews of his book by six different critics of the same importance! No two of them agree upon his worth, his characterization, his style, his power to interest, his prospects. There is nothing for him to do but sit back and reflect that all criticism is individual opinion. Let him also recall that a man named Rogers was considered a greater poet than Byron during the lifetime of both, that 'Wuthering Heights' was ignored for thirty years, that Conrad was known only to the *cognoscenti* of the United States until Mencken beat the big drum.

Bring to fruition whatever sprouts in your fiction tract, express yourself in your own way, do your best, take your chances. No use to try to please anyone but yourself — unless, to be sure, you would write Mush for Morons. Even then you might not succeed, for success in this field is said not to be as simple as it sounds.

Having myself written novels of two different *genres* — modern and historical — I unhesitatingly cast my vote for the historical. This, be it understood, is purely personal, not didactic. I have derived a thousand times more pleasure from writing of the past, even if only a generation away, than of the life about me. It is paradoxical that I am an avid newspaper reader and follow current events in the magazines and reviews with the same interest, but this I am unable to explain. I read every line of news from Russia, for instance, but nothing would induce me to read another Russian novel, not even one by James Hilton. No news is more absorbing than what I hear on the radio or read in the newspapers about Washington, but even a mystery story whose stage is set in Washington bores me. Also, I find the problems of Labor vs. Capital, strikes, communism, Big Business, Depression, intensely interesting in my morning and evening paper, but boring beyond words as subjects of fiction.

To save myself correspondence I hasten to answer the question: Why then did you ever write contemporaneous novels if you felt yourself better equipped to write the historical, and found more pleasure in haunting the past? I might answer: Why did you marry the wrong woman (or man), or why have you done a thousand and one things in your life that you only half-wanted to do? But I will be polite and explain as well as I know how. Save for a few amateur performances, which I ignore, I began by writing historical novels and stories, even if only of the preceding generation — for those at least were social history — and had every intention of doing nothing else. I liked the perspective, the research, the re-creation of a past era. But partly because someone piqued me by saying that I was not in tune with my own times and never would be: that I was born too late or too soon; partly because in due course, that is to say in a wider experience of life, contemporaneous stories would suddenly begin to prowl about my fiction tract; partly because earlier in my career not enough historical characters appealed to me — there was an interval of four years between 'The Conqueror' and 'Rezanov,' and then nineteen years passed before 'The Immortal Marriage' — just about half of my output has dealt with the passing scene. Even so, I have been accused of making my contemporary heroines 'superwomen' — although what my critics meant was *un*-ordinary — just as I chose superwomen of history, like Aspasia, to resurrect. Well, I hate commonplace persons both in fiction and out; so that is that. What I am looking for is more superwomen in history. But I am advising no one to follow my example.

I have also been reproached for not writing novels that would help the average woman to solve her problems. My answer to that is: Any woman who can't solve her own problems without the help of fiction is a poor stick, and I for one shall not waste a penful of ink over her.

GERTRUDE STEIN

I have made the discovery that sentences are not emotional and that paragraphs are.

LORD DUNSANY

I think I owe most of my style to the reports of proceedings in the divorce court.

WILLIAM McFEE

Most American writing conveys the impression of a ride on the subway in the rush hour.

JOSEPH HERGESHEIMER

I've got to the point where I can't stand novels. I don't read them.

H. L. MENCKEN

The impulse to create beauty is rather rare in literary men.

J. B. PRIESTLEY

The 'stream of consciousness' method of novel writing always reminds me of some slatternly woman who slops about the house all day in kimono and bedroom slippers.

HAVELOCK ELLIS believes that style is an affirmation of the writer's personality, not a sheet of glass in which all that matters is the absence of flaws.

THE ARTIST IN WORDS

A BOOK in any worthy sense, as I conceive it, is a personal expression of the writer's mind. Writing is not necessarily this. To write may simply be to convey information or news. So that a school manual is not in this sense a book, and journalism is not of the same texture as a book.

We recognise a book in this sense by its individual style. If the writer is expressing his individual self, he cannot help revealing, however little he may be thinking of this, a personal style.

In this way every writer has his own music, though there are few in whom it becomes audible save at rare and precious intervals. The great writers, though they are always themselves, attain the perfect music of their style under the stress of a stimulus adequate to arouse it. Their music is the audible translation of emotion, and only arises when the waves of emotion are stirred. It is not properly speaking a voluntary effect. We can but say that the winds of the spirit are breathed upon the surface of style, and they lift it into rhythmic movement. And for each writer these waves have their own special rate of vibration, their peculiar shape and interval. The rich, deep, slow tones of Bacon have nothing in common with the haunting, long-drawn melody, faint and tremulous, of Newman; the high metallic falsetto ring of De Quincey's rhetoric is far away from the pensive low-toned music of Pater.

As a writer slowly finds his own centre of gravity, the influence of the rhythm of other writers ceases to be perceptible except in so far as it coincides with his own natural movement and *tempo*. That is a familiar fact. We less easily realise, perhaps, that not only the tunes but the notes that they are formed of are, in every great writer, his own. In other words, he creates even his vocabulary. If we examine the style of Montaigne, so fresh and personal and inventive, we see that its originality lies largely in its vocabulary, which is not, like that of Rabelais, manufactured afresh, but has its novelty in its metaphorical values, such new values being tried and tempered at every step, to the measure of the highly individual person behind them, who thereby exerts his creative force. In later days Huysmans, who indeed saw the world at a more eccentric angle than Montaigne, yet with unflinching veracity and absolute devotion, set himself to the task of creating his own vocabulary, and at first the unfamiliarity of its beauty estranges us.

To think of Huysmans is to be led towards an aspect of style not to be passed over. To say that the artist in words is expressing a new vision of the world and seeking the designations for things as he sees them, is a large part of the truth, and, I would say, perhaps the most important part of it. He finds that words have a rich content of their own, they are alive and they flourish or decay. They send out connecting threads in every direction, they throb with meaning that ever changes and reverberates afar. The writer is not always, or often, merely preparing a *catalogue raisonné* of things, he is an artist and his pigments are words. Often he merely takes his suggestions from the things of the world and makes his own pictures without any real resemblance to the scene it is supposed to depict. Dujardin tells us that he once took Huysmans to a Wagner concert; he scarcely listened to the music, but he was fascinated by the programme the attendant handed to him; he went home to write a brilliant page on 'Tannhäuser.' Mallarmé, on the other hand, was soaked in music; to him music was the voice of the world, and it was the aim of poetry to express the world by itself becoming music; he stood on a height like a pioneer and looked towards the Promised Land, trying to catch intimations of a new sensibility and a future art.

Even the greatest writers are affected by the intoxication of mere words in the artistry of language. Shakespeare is, constantly, and, not content with 'making the green one red,' he must needs at the same time 'the multitudinous seas incarnadine.' It is conspicuous in Keats, and often, as in 'The Eve of St. Agnes,' where he seemed to be concerned with beautiful things, he was really concerned with beautiful words. In that way he is sometimes rather misleading for the too youthful reader; 'porphyry' seemed to me a marvellous substance when as a boy of twelve I read of it in Keats, and I imagine that Keats himself would have been surprised, had he lived long enough to walk to St. Thomas's Hospital over the new London Bridge, when told that he was treading a granite that was porphyritic. I recall how Verlaine would sometimes repeat in varying tones some rather unfamiliar word, rolling it round and round in his mouth, sucking it like a sweetmeat, licking the sound into the shape that pleased him; some people may perhaps have found a little bizarre the single words ('Green,' for example) which he sometimes made the title of a song, but if they adopt the preliminary Verlainian process they may understand how he had fitted such words to music and meaning.

The artist in speech thus moves among words rather than among things. Words are closely related to things, but in their far reverberation they have become enriched by many associations, saturated with many colours; they have acquired a life of their own, moving on another plane than that of things, and it is on that plane that the artist in words is, as an artist, concerned with them.

It so comes about that the artist in words, like the artist in pigments, is perpetually passing between two planes — the plane of new vision and the plane of new creation. He is sometimes remoulding the external world and sometimes the internal world; sometimes, by predilection, lingering more on one plane than on the other plane. The artist in words is not irresistibly drawn to the exact study of things or moved by the strong love of Nature. The poets who describe Nature most minutely and most faithfully are not usually the great poets. That is intelligible because the poet — even the poet in the wide sense who also uses prose — is primarily the instrument of human emotion and not of scientific observation. Yet that poet possesses immense resources of strength who in early life has stored within him the minute knowledge of some field of the actual external world. One may doubt, indeed, whether there has been any supreme poet, from Homer on, who has not had this inner reservoir of sensitive impressions to draw from. The youthful Shakespeare who wrote the poems, with their minute descriptions, was not a great poet, as the youthful Marlowe was, but he was storing up the material which, when he had developed into a great poet, he could draw on at need with a careless and assured hand. Without such reservoirs, the novelists also would never attain to that touch of the poet which, beyond their story-telling power, can stir our hearts. 'À la Recherche du Temps Perdu' is the name of a great modern book, but every novelist during part of his time has been a Ulysses on a perilous voyage of adventure for that far home. One thinks of George Eliot and her early intimacy with the life of country people, of Hardy who had acquired so acute a sensitivity to the sounds of Nature, of Conrad who had caught the flashes of penetrating vision which came to the sailor on deck. In so far as they move away into scenes where they cannot draw from those ancient reservoirs, the adventures of these artists, however brilliant they may become, lose their power of intimate appeal.

We grow familiar in time with the style of the great writers, and when we read them we translate them easily and unconsciously, as we translate a foreign language we are familiar with; we understand the vocabulary because we have learnt to know the special seal of the creative person who moulded the vocabulary. But at the outset the great writer may be almost as unintelligible to us as though he were writing in a language we had never learnt. In the now remote days when 'Leaves of Grass' was a new book in the world, few who looked into it for the first time, however honestly, but were repelled and perhaps even violently repelled, and it is hard to realise now that once those who fell on Swinburne's 'Poems and Ballads' saw at first only picturesque hieroglyphics to which they had no key. But even today how many there are who find Proust unreadable and Joyce unintelligible. Until we find the door and the clue the new writer remains obscure. Therein lies the truth of Landor's saying that the poet must himself create the beings who are to enjoy his Paradise.

For most of those who deliberately seek to learn to write, words seem generally to be felt as of less importance than the art of arranging them. It is thus that the learner in writing tends to become the devoted student of grammar and syntax whom we came across at the outset. That is indeed a tendency which always increases. Civilisation develops with a conscious adhesion to formal order, and the writer — writing by fashion or by ambition and not by divine right of creative instinct — follows the course of civilisation. It is an unfortunate tendency, for those whom it affects conquer by their number. As we know, writing that is real is not learnt that way. Just as the solar system was not made in accordance with the astronomer's laws, so writing is not made by the laws of grammar. Astronomer and grammarian alike can only come in at the end, to give a generalised description of what usually happens in the respective fields it pleases them to explore. When a new comet, cosmic or literary, enters their sky, it is their descriptions which have to be readjusted, and not the comet. There seems to be no more pronounced mark of the decadence of a people and its literature than a servile and rigid subserviency to rule. It can only make for ossification, for anchylosis, for petrification, all the milestones on the road of death. In every age of democratic plebeianism, where each man thinks he is as good a writer as the others, and takes his laws from the others, having no laws of his own nature, it is down this steep path that men, in a flock, inevitably run.

There can be no doubt that in the matter of style we have paid heavily for the attainment of our slavish adherence to mechanical rules, however convenient, however inevitable. The beautiful incorrection, as we are now compelled to regard it, that so often marked the great and even the small writers of the seventeenth century, has been lost, for all can now write what any find it easy to read, what none have any consuming desire to read. But when Sir Thomas Browne wrote his 'Religio Medici' it was with an art made up of obedience to personal law and abandonment to free inspiration which still ravishes us. It is extraordinary how far indifference or incorrection of style may be carried and yet remain completely adequate even to complex and subtle ends. Pepys wrote his 'Diary,' at the outset of a life full of strenuous work and not a little pleasure, with a rare devotion indeed, but with a concision and carelessness, a single eye on the fact itself, and an extraordinary absence of self-consciousness which rob it of all claim to possess what we conventionally term style. Yet in this vehicle he has perfectly conveyed not merely the most vividly realised and delightfully detailed picture of a past age ever achieved in any language, but he has, moreover, painted a psychological portrait of himself which for its serenely impartial justice, its subtle gradations, its bold juxtapositions of colours, has all the qualities of the finest Velasquez. There is no style here, we say, merely the diarist, writing with careless poignant vitality for his own eye, and yet no style that we could conceive would be better fitted, or so well fitted, for the miracle that has here been effected.

The personal freedom of Browne led up to splendour, and that of Pepys to clarity. But while splendour is not the whole of writing, neither, although one returns to it again and again, is clarity. Here we come from another side on to a point we had already reached. Bergson, in reply to the question: 'Comment doivent écrire les Philosophes?' lets fall some observations, which, as he himself remarks, concern other writers beside philosophers. A technical word, he remarks, even a word invented for the occasion or used in a special sense, is always in place provided the instructed reader — though the difficulty, as he fails to point out, is to be sure of possessing this instructed reader — accepts it so easily as not even to notice it, and he proceeds to say that in philosophic prose, and in all prose, and indeed in all the arts, 'the perfect expression is that which has come so naturally, or rather so necessarily, by virtue of so imperious a predestination, that we do not pause before it, but go straight on to what it seeks to express, as though it were blended with the idea; it became invisible by force of being transparent.' That is well said. Bergson also is on the side of clarity. Yet I do not feel that that is all there is to say. Style is not a sheet of glass in which the only thing that matters is the absence of flaws. Style indeed is not really a mere invisible transparent medium, it is not really a garment, but, as Gourmont said, the very thought itself. It is the miraculous transubstantiation of a spiritual body, given to us in the only form in which we may receive and absorb that body, and unless its clarity is balanced by its beauty it is not adequate to sustain that most high function.

As a part of the harmony of art, which is necessarily made out of conflict, we have to view that perpetual seeming alternation between the two planes — the plane of vision and the plane of creation, the form within and the garment that clothes it — which may sometimes distract the artist himself. The prophet Ezekiel once said (and modern prophets have doubtless had occasion to recognise the truth of his remark) that he seemed to the people round him only as 'one that hath a pleasant voice and can play well on an instrument.' But he failed to understand that it was only through this quality of voice and instrument that his exhortations had any vital force or even any being, and that if the poem goes the message goes. Indeed, that is true of all his fellow prophets of the Old Testament and the New who have fascinated mankind with the sound of those harps that they had once hung by the waters of Babylon. We cannot but follow the piper that knows how to play, even to our own destruction. There may be much that is objectionable about Man. But he has that engaging trait. And the world will end when he has lost it.

The freedom of art by no means involves the easiness of art. It may rather, indeed, be said the difficulty increases with freedom, for to make things in accordance with patterns is ever the easiest task. The problem is equally arduous for those who, so far as their craft is conscious, seek an impersonal and for those who seek a personal ideal of style. Flaubert sought — in vain, it is true — to be the most objective of artists and to mould speech with heroic energy in shapes of abstract perfection. Nietzsche, one of the most personal artists in style, sought also, in his own words, to work at a page of prose as a sculptor works at a statue. Though the result is not perhaps fundamentally different, whichever ideal it is that, consciously or instinctively, is followed, the personal road of style is doubtless theoretically — though not necessarily in practice — the sounder, usually also that which moves most of us more profoundly. The great prose writers of the Second Empire in France made an unparalleled effort to carve or paint impersonal prose, but its final beauty and effectiveness seem scarcely equal to the splendid energy it embodies. Jules de Goncourt, his brother thought, literally died from the mental exhaustion of his unceasing struggle to attain an objective style adequate to express the subtle texture of the world as he saw it. But, while the Goncourts are great figures in literary history, they have pioneered no new road, nor are they of the writers whom men continuously love to read; for it is simply as a document that the 'Journal' remains of enduring value.

Yet the great writers of any school bear witness, each in his own way, that, deeper than these conventions and decorums of style, there is a law which no writer can escape from, a law which must needs be learnt, but can never be taught. That is the law of the logic of thought. All the conventional rules of the construction of speech may be put aside if a writer is thereby enabled to follow more closely and lucidly the form and process of his thought. It is the law of that logic that he must for ever follow and in attaining it alone find rest. All progress in literary style lies in the heroic resolve to cast aside accretions and exuberances, all the conventions of a past age that were once beautiful because alive and are now false because dead. The simple and naked beauty of Swift's style, sometimes so keen and poignant, rests absolutely on this truth to the logic of his thought. The twin qualities of flexibility and intimacy are of the essence of all progress in the art of language, and in their progressive achievement lies the attainment of great literature. If we compare Shakespeare with his predecessors and contemporaries, we can scarcely say that in imaginative force he is vastly superior to Marlowe, or in intellectual grip to Jonson, but he immeasurably surpasses them in flexibility and in intimacy. He was able with an incomparable art to weave a garment of speech so flexible in its strength, so intimate in its transparence, that it lent itself to every shade of emotion and the quickest turns of thought. All the writers who influence those who come after them have done so by the same method. They have thrown aside the awkward and outworn garments of speech, they have woven a simpler and more familiar speech, able to express subtleties or audacities that before seemed inexpressible. That was once done in English verse by Cowper and Wordsworth, in English prose by Addison and Lamb. That has been done in French today by Proust and in English by Joyce.

No doubt it is possible for a writer to go far by the exercise of a finely attentive docility. By a dutiful study of what other people have said, by a refined cleverness in catching their tricks, and avoiding their subtleties, their profundities, their audacities, by, in short, a patient perseverance in writing out copper-plate maxims in elegant copybooks, he can become at last, like Stevenson, the idol of the crowd. But the great writer can only learn out of himself. He learns to write as a child learns to walk. For the laws of the logic of thought are not other than those of physical movement. There is stumbling, awkwardness, hesitation, experiment — before at last the learner attains the perfect command of that divine rhythm and perilous poise in which he asserts his supreme human privilege. But the process of his learning rests ultimately on his own structure and function and not on others' example. 'Style must be founded upon models'; it is the rule set up by the pedant who knows nothing of what style means. For the style that is founded on a model is the negation of style.

The ardour and heroism of great achievement in style never grow less as the ages pass, but rather tend to grow more. That is so, not merely because the hardest tasks are left for the last, but because of the ever increasing impediments placed in the path of style by the piling up of mechanical rules and rigid conventions. It is doubtful whether on the whole the forces of life really gain on the surrounding inertia of death. The greatest writers must spend the blood and sweat of their souls, amid the execration and disdain of their contemporaries, in breaking the old moulds of style and pouring their fresh life into new moulds. From Dante to Carducci, from Rabelais to Proust, from Chaucer to Whitman, the giants of letters have been engaged in this life-giving task, and behind them the forces of death swiftly gather again. Here there is always room for the hero. No man, indeed, can write anything that matters who is not a hero at heart, even though to the people who pass him in the street or know him in the house he may seem as gentle as any dove. If all progress lies in an ever greater flexibility and intimacy of speech, a finer adaptation to the heights and depths of the mobile human soul, the task can never be finally completed. Every writer is called afresh to reveal new strata of life. By digging in his own soul he becomes the discoverer of the soul of his family, of his nation, of the race, of the heart of humanity. For the great writer finds style as the mystic finds God, in his own soul. It is the final utterance of a sigh, which none could utter before him, and which all can who follow.

Writing is an arduous spiritual and intellectual task, only to be achieved by patient and deliberate labour and much daring. Yet therewith we are only at the beginning. Writing is also the expression of individual personality, which springs up spontaneously, or is slowly drawn up from within, out of a well of inner emotions which none may command. But even with these two opposite factors we have not attained the complete synthesis. For style in the full sense is more than the deliberate and designed creation, more even than the unconscious and involuntary creation, of the individual man who therein expresses himself. The self that he thus expresses is a bundle of inherited tendencies that came the man himself can never entirely know whence. It is by the instinctive stress of a highly sensitive or slightly abnormal constitution, that he is impelled to instil these tendencies into the alien magic of words.

So, in the end, we come back to the point from which we started: a book in any worthy sense is the personal expression of its writer. The art is essential — that is why we must bring in the conception of worth or value — but the primary and fundamental necessity is an impelling passion.

There are writers — quite as frequently found in America as elsewhere — who approach the making of a book with the temperament of the craftsman and nothing more. They may painfully produce what looks at first like a work of art. But it has no vitality, it is seen to be pastiche, it speedily withers. Even when it is not pastiche, the ultimate end must be the same. Joyce in his later writings is even more inventive and artful than Rabelais in the matter of verbal texture. But beneath that texture in Rabelais we are conscious of a great spirit striving to suggest the great conceptions he cannot openly express. So we read him today. But we do not feel confident that the fascinating gibberish of the later Joyce will be read in the same spirit four centuries hence. Artfulness or art, it is not enough.

Yet neither is the passion alone enough. D. H. Lawrence was not greatly concerned to produce art, and to be an artist was not his supreme aim. He was concerned to express his ideas, which for him were of immense importance. But today his ideas seem for the most part incoherent, confused, fundamentally incomprehensible. He regarded himself as only incidentally an artist. Yet it is as an artist that he survives.

Would you write a book? Follow the guidance of your passion. Yet, be very sure that, unless in following that guidance you become, consciously or unconsciously, an artist, you will not in any worthy sense have written a book.

FANNIE HURST

I'm not happy when I'm writing, but I'm more unhappy when I'm not.

SINCLAIR LEWIS

Writing is dirty work.

GEORGE MOORE

It is incredible the trouble I have to take to produce even a passable sentence that other men write unthinkingly.

HILAIRE BELLOC

I hate my trade.

JAMES BRANCH CABELL

There is, in brief, no more dreadful reading for any honest writer than he must find in his own books, after a while.

WILBUR DANIEL STEELE

There is a time when a tale is a fine and beautiful creature, a masterpiece without flaw; and that is just before you sit down to write it.

MARY AGNES HAMILTON
*states the case for that 'second-line'
army of writers who hear the voices
of angels yet stutter in reporting them.*

THE WILL TO WRITE

I

BOOKS, of course, are like people — 'so many, and so many, and such glee!' One looks round one's shelves, and greets friends and companions: sees faces that, although so distinct and individual, yet look one thing to me, another to you; personalities that, like those of flesh and blood, come out fully only in response to some answering quality in their interlocutor. They communicate the experiences which have helped to make them, and which, in turn, they help to make for readers; they do this, indeed, so richly and so fully that there are times when it is difficult to disentangle what one has seen with one's own eyes, and what had shown one, by their printed pages. So much like people are they that to think of making one is to assume a Godlike faculty. One hesitates and asks — Am I entitled to do this?

One hesitates the more when one compares the mastery that has conceived, formed, coloured, infused with life the great books of the world's literature with the limited capacity that is one's own portion. It is the experience, I am sure, of many writers of novels, as it is my own, that while absorbed in the effort to get one's own thing into shape, one must abstain from reading the works of others. Henry James, for example, that long and lovely row of treasure-houses has to stand there, locked against one's enjoyment. He is too 'catching' — and that in the wrong way. If one could 'catch' his mind, good, wonderful, but there is no hope of that; what one does 'catch' is his turn of sentence, his trick with adverb and adjective: and that, at second-hand, is neither good nor wonderful. There is, moreover, always the danger that, if one seeks to refresh oneself with the pages that really *are* pages, one lays them down again with a sick revulsion against those one has just written, and is faced with that dark, accusatory question, Why write badly when others write well?

It is a bad moment this; and it recurs. I want here to face it, and to answer the question, if I can, as one of those who, without anything that could be called full artistic justification, has yet every intention of going on writing. My excuse is that I am, here, representative of what is, after all, by far the largest block of 'artists,' whether the instrument of effort be the pen, the brush, the chisel, the piano, the fiddle, or the voice; whether they take their stand on the platform or the stage or in the bookseller's window, face their critics on the boards or between them.

Criticism, whether higher or normal, is apt for its own purposes to assume but two groups of artists, whether creative or executive — the group of genius and the group of commerce. Any such demarcation, however, leaves out the vast majority of actual artists. Its rough-and-ready test is performance, intention is neglected, overlooked. That, however, makes the division as false in application, and as a guide to apprehension, as would be a judicial procedure which took no account of motive. It does not fit the case. Take novels. Every reader is aware of a distinction to be drawn quite different from this: a distinction between the novels which are, to phrase it quite crudely, 'trying to be good' and those which are not. Every reviewer worth his salt pays homage to this distinction. He recognizes the writer who has a sense of craftsmanship and an appreciation of its possibilities, even when that sense goes far beyond his power to do what he sees; he treats such work seriously, as he ought. He knows, too, that for one artist who can do what he sees, there are ten who can see but not do, fully, or to their own satisfaction, yet, what they see.

This sense of a standard, this respect for a craft is, of course, confused by the perpetual tendency, in any given period, which causes artists, like other people, to adopt whatever method, approach, and scale of values happen to be in vogue. There are always, of course, the merely 'clever' performers, who neither see nor try to see below the contemporary surface, and adapt, without scruple, the trick of contemporary vision and handling. Even of them not all by any means are insincere; it is one of the many odd phenomena of this odd world we inhabit that, just as persons are born with the physical shape and face that happens, at the hour, to be in fashion — every woman at one moment slim, tall, flat: at another, curvy and rosy: the Burne-Jones face, the Botticelli face, the Augustus John face appearing in nature as they have done in art — so the individuals in whom the queer itch for artistic expression of some sort is innate also tend to appear with heads, and mental and moral furniture in those heads, of the modish shape. As their period thinks, and sees, and forms, so do they, naturally, think and see and form. The moral and intellectual outfit of the day suits them, as do its clothes and hats; indeed it would be more accurate to phrase the case as is done by the Scots, and say that they suit these ideas and these clothes. This certainly is a fascinating problem, and not least for those who happen not to be of the right shape; who do not suit their period. But it must not be allowed to mask or blur the real distinction — that between those who have, and those who have not, the craftsman's sense for the loyal use of his material.

This is half of the characteristic equipment of the artist. It is possessed, to their joy and grief, by many writers, musicians and painters, whose actual performances nevertheless register their failure so to use their instrument as to realize and release fully what they have in their minds. They are aware, with a clarity no critic can approach, of the gap in their own case between vision and execution; they judge their own performances with a harsh realism no one else can bring to them. Yet the very sense of that gap, of that failure, keeps them trying. It keeps them trying; but it also keeps them impaled on a grim uncertainty. They cannot help writing, painting or composing. Yet while the drive to work is strong enough to keep them doing it, it is yet not so strong or so secure that the question does not arise, in their minds, Why? Why do not very well what others have done, and a few are now doing, supremely well?

When practitioners discuss this issue among themselves, a curious fact emerges. Writers are, as a rule, clear that there is no room for the second-line musician or painter; painters are equally clear that there is no room for the second-line writer or musician; musicians are clear that there is no room for the second-line writer or painter. Yet these same writers, musicians and painters will defend the second-line artists in their own domain, and that not out of mere politeness. I incline to think that the defence is right, the attack wrong.

Admittedly, my own feelings are here involved. I am a member of the second-line army; and typical of it. Therefore, my statement of its case will, much as I dislike writing in 'I,' have to be largely personal. I am not going to take refuge behind any bush of assembly, nor am I going to be ambiguous or indistinct on either half of the equation: neither, that is to say, about my sense of artistic inadequacy, on the one hand, nor about my determination to go on writing, on the other. This co-existence of critical awareness and unaffected determination to persist is the point of interest; I present my case simply as representative.

II

I do not think that there has ever been a time when, had the Good Fairy of the story-books appeared to me with gifts in her hand and one, of my own selection, designed for me, I should not have asked her to give me the power to write, to write something about which I could, in my own mind, be sure that it was absolutely good. That desire still under-runs every other, as it has persisted through every other. It has moved in me, ever since I was a small child. I was, like so many other children, writing a History of My Dolls at seven or eight, and issuing a weekly paper, wholly written and illustrated by myself, at ten. Yet there never has been a time, from the moment at which I could form my letters, when I have not been displeased by the sight of the calligraphy in which I yet ardently cover page after page, or not dissatisfied with the substance and the manner of what I produced in that same unpleasing script. (I type, if anything, rather worse than I write and never type except under economic compulsion.) I have never yet satisfied my own standard of workmanship, when, over a gap in time, I look back over what I have written. At the time, I often, of course, feel, 'This is good'; there are chapters and pages that please me; but that sense of serene achievement I should have begged of the Fairy — No.

As with most writers, my critical faculty is strong. It was early developed and trained by contact with minds much better than my own, as with the masterpieces of the world's literature. It is and has always been better, more subtle, much more accurate, more reliable, in every way stronger, than my creative faculty. Instinctively, I have always known this. About the faults and weaknesses of my writing, and wherein they consist, there is little that anyone can tell me. The moments at which anything I have done has seemed to me good, truthful, fully expressive, even surprising, stand out, as high lights in my experience. Their pure and intense joy is unique. But they have been paid for by others. Then, impelled from within or from without, the contrary conviction has seized me with force, and held me rigid in a misery in its own way as acute and as possessive. This swing, especially on its lower half, has so far as I know, not yet been treated with the painful fullness it deserves, in anybody's fiction. It is one of the multitudinous subjects that await handling; perhaps one day I shall make a mess of it myself. If I do, I shall try to render the sensations of the two years in my life on which I most dislike to look back. I was then working with an editor, himself an admirable master of English, although devoid of constructive illumination, who, definitely and positively, disliked my writing, and had no hesitation in letting me know it. He certainly taught me something — although not, as he designed, to stop trying; but the constant sense of defeat, humiliation, and bafflement, and the fundamental doubts I then endured, brought me nearer to understanding the impulse of the suicide than I have ever been. Literally, it was as bad as that. I can see him, now, looking with disgust at a piece of copy, started by me with bright enthusiasm and worked over with infinite pains, and then proceeding to rewrite it until little or nothing of the original survived. Some relief came when I realized that he disliked not only my writing but the things I wanted to say: that he sought to give me not only a new nib to my pen (failing the better result — my throwing pen away altogether) but a new shape to my mind. On that realization — since, whatever I thought of my nib, I did prefer the shape of my mind to his — I released myself. I forced an issue on a matter of policy for the paper, and, by driving him to take up a position I knew, and he knew that I knew, to be false, restored my self-respect. But, had I stayed on in that office for another year, I doubt if I could have survived. The power to go on trying to write would have been broken.

This experience — or experiences in essence similar — has, of course, been tasted in gulps since. Never again, however, has it been, as for those two years it was, my daily diet. I am not going here further to inspect the highly interesting distress caused the artist by his own failure in performance, though it is that which hurts. The critic from without merely rubs it in, and can, I suppose, assuage it, may even, in particular cases, numb it out of action. What a success which the inner standard knows to be undeserved is like, I do not know; nor am I suggesting that success is, as a rule, achieved without desert. I don't think it is. But what I am here concerned to investigate is something different, and, to me, more interesting still: the resilient element that insists on reasserting itself: insists, that is, on making one go on trying to do better next time, what I know I have not done well enough this time. Here, the second-line artist is the supreme exemplar of the faith that is a perpetually conquered doubt. Of that I am a specimen; I emerged from my editor's office, harder set than ever on learning how to write; I was writing a book of my own throughout the period during which he was trying — and that with genuine skill and persistency, and a very good case at his back — to break me of the habit. He came near to doing it, but, so soon as I got out from under, I finished that book and have written several since. He no doubt despises them, and me; it makes no difference.

What is it that thus keeps one going? Partly, of course, it is something quite simple. Trying is fun — the greatest fun there is. A form of fun that, in its course, may carry vexation, distress, humiliation, at moments, something very near despair, but never permits of boredom. That dread spectre is banished. One is not, at bottom, bored with oneself — since one is going on trying; one is not bored with the world. Compared to the steady, standing, holding fascination of this effort, how pallid is the appeal of bridge, the crossword puzzle, or of any sport or game yet invented. When A. E. Housman said there was 'no harm' in trying, he was actually thinking of cricket —

> 'Try I will, no harm in trying;
> Wonder 'tis how little mirth
> Keeps the bones of men from lying
> On the bed of earth...'

Cricket, absorbing as it is, and rich in the joyous effort to be better at it than one is, has nothing like the resources, for that purpose, of writing. Its field of survey, of effort, of understanding, of perception is limited: as limited as is its season, confined to the summer. Writing, on the other hand, for the writer joins on to everything, illuminates everything, enlarges and vivifies the winter as fully as the summer of the soul. Everyone he meets, everything he hears or sees, everywhere he goes fits in and may irradiate his experience. The state of mind of a novelist, for example, when he is 'well in' on a novel, with the characters alive for him, and the action-pieces assembled and only waiting for him to arrange them and fit them into their intrinsically determined pattern, is one of the richest and most various bliss. Then, he is a king, with none of the drawbacks and all the privileges of absolute sovereignty. Above all, he has a sense of easy mastery over a world, which, in turn, enriches and illuminates the actual, visible world of his daily life. Every experience, however small, however large, then joins on to his engrossing theme. For him there is no lost motion, no wasted time, no missed connections. The dullest journey, the dreariest committee, the stupidest party — all bring him nourishment. He is then, as Henry James puts it, one of those 'on whom nothing is lost'; he is, or imagines himself to be, 'finely aware and richly responsible.' Then the devastating question, Why am I here? has no terrors, raises no howling echoes. He knows. If, like the hero of so many fictions, he were to be told that he has but three weeks or three months to live, he would know what to do with them. He would simply glue himself to his desk and there sit writing until he had finished his novel.

It is fun. It is the greatest fun there is. Such fun that, while one is at it, nothing can spoil its delight or shear it of a unique quality. The toil is long: the delight brief. The naïve illusion with which one finishes a first novel does not recur; its untainted certainty has a completeness hardly experienced again. As the toll of writings behind one piles up, knowledge of the inevitable after-taste does, a little, mar the delicious flavour of present accomplishment; coming comparison between the botch one has made and the bright beauty more skilful hands could extract out of similar material does cast an early shadow on enjoyment. Yet to each book there attach moments of glow; these moments do, still, carry conviction with them that, however brief that glow may be, it is in kind different from that accompanying any other pleasure whatsoever; as, if evanescent, nevertheless real.

To that conviction I cling. It is, for the answer to the question, Why write badly when others write well? Only by and in writing does one get this special and peculiar sense of glow, which is at once the most personal thing one has and the most disinterested. It is independent of, and not derived from, any sense of self-satisfaction; so much so, that even acute personal dissatisfaction cannot kill it. It comes, or seems to come, *to* one, not *from* one. It carries with it, as essential part of it, an awareness of the not-self. That awareness, so hard to define, so difficult to convey, so impossible not to feel, is its core; and it is a core of light and warmth. Whether or no what one has written conveys it to others, or seems to register it fully to oneself, while one is writing one does *see*. So vivid and so authentic is this sense of perception, of apprehension, even of vision that to render and so fully 'get' it seems by far the most important and significant aspect of one's existence. It is what one is 'for.' So much what one is for that no series of admitted previous partial defeats can prevent one from again giving all one has to the effort, this time, to get it right. Nothing that one sees through the eyes of others, or takes, more or less passively, at second-hand, has anything like the authority of the vision one then struggles to express in words.

Voir, c'est avoir. That there is something to see and to show, no writer whatever be his professed, intellectual, and non-professional opinions, can, as writer, doubt. The fact that he does go on writing is witness, beyond any argument of his, beyond any negativism to which he may be expressly dedicated, to this faith. Take a case as formidable, from this point of view, as that of Mr. Somerset Maugham. Professionally, he is a craftsman of such eminence that doubts as to the security of his own performance may well not visit him; but were his cynical professions about human nature and the universal chaos in which it is set to be taken at their face value he ought, out of this far-ranging disbelief, to write nothing. Yet he writes. He would, no doubt, say that thereby he earns his living. But that is not the true answer. He writes because he cannot help it; he wants to express, to order, to make something that he sees. Were he really the whole-hearted 'No' man that he presents, he would not write; it would plainly not be worth while; he would 'refuse the ticket.' As it is, he is willy-nilly, 'a witness to the Lord.'

Here, incidentally, is the simple and sufficient justification for the popular view that writers are somehow 'romantic' persons, and writing, however much those who do it may groan and grumble, a romantic business. To that much-abused word, true significance is thus given back. I remember reading, some years ago now, a notice in the Literary Supplement of the London *Times* of the 'Diary of Eugene Delacroix' — incidentally one of the most fascinating books ever written, and the most revealing of the mind of the artist. The writer of the review was evidently puzzled by something in the outlook and the experience of this eminently romantic painter. After noting, with surprise, that the chief 'events' in his life were certain journeys, notably in Morocco and the Far East, he went on to say, 'For there was, apparently, no romance in the life of this Romantic, no love-affair, no marriage even, no difficulty of any sort save the difficulty of becoming a master in one's art.'

I have always cherished this sentence, since, apart from its delicious reference to 'no love-affair, no marriage even,' it contains, so neatly and concisely wrapped up together, the wrong view and the right view about romance. The wrong view — I put it quite dogmatically, since there is no room here for expansion on this theme — is that romance is an aspect of sexual attraction *per se:* that it attaches to any and every love-affair, and 'even,' though in lesser degree, to marriage. This is plain nonsense. Everyone can see how nonsensical it is if he regards the love-affairs of his friends; few, very few, of them suggest any gleam of that sense of wonder which is of the essence of romance. Delacroix felt that wonder in painting and in the vision which his painting sought to render and create; what is romantic about him is precisely his absorption in the 'difficulty of becoming a master in one's art.' Every artist who sticks to the effort after that mastery is, to that extent, romantic, since what keeps him stuck is his sense of the wonder that he may hold if he achieves it, and sees in proportion as he strives for it. For the writer, it is the wonder of the word made flesh.

Artists may be, although by no means all of them are or have been, persons of many love-affairs. To that extent their conviction has broken and betrayed them; they have sought to find the beauty to which their art might lead them in some merely human companion. It is not then, but when they are struggling to be 'masters in their art' that they are in truth romantic; at their desk or at their easel, rather than at the bedside, wonder wreathes their heads.

I am not suggesting, nor do I believe, that there is any hard-

and-fast line to be drawn between the seeing of the artist and the sympathetic perception the ordinary man brings to an achieved work of art. They are part of a series. As Professor Alexander has put it: 'The artist is not an exception to the common run, but merely a specially gifted member of the community, whose gifts lead him into artistic expression. Just so the saint would be a mystery were not the common run of mankind religious.' The impulse to make, like the desire to see, is general and not special. The artist feels, at a higher potency, something in its nature common. *Quâ* craftsman he is distinct; but he belongs, there too, to a vast army of potential craftsmen, in materials covering the widest range from pen to hammer and pick. What is individual in him is the alignment of more than normally intense perception and experience to a given medium for its expression and communication.

To the writer, experience translates itself into and achieves reality through words; to the painter, through visual images; to the musician, through sound sequences. This alliance to, and dependence on, his given material is, in the make-up of the artist, central. Content, for him, exists in relation to a given form, a given material. The trick of contemporary criticism to praise or dispraise novels, for example, in terms of painting or of music, is therefore quite inept. Everyone recognizes in himself a more marked sensibility to artistic enjoyment through some particular form, some specialized sense; notes that he receives impressions more readily through eye or ear; through words or sound or lines. In the artist, this specialization is carried very much further. The practice of his own chosen art does, of course, heighten his general sensibility; but he reacts to great impressions in terms of his chosen and inevitable material. To make a novel of them is as surely the impulse of the novelist as to make a picture is that of the painter. The writer gives them in words: he also takes them most readily in that form. He sees; but his seeing cannot occur in a void nor in the vague; seeing becomes possession when its substance has been expressed in words.

'Art,' said Moussorgsky, 'is communication between man and man.' Deep in the artist is lodged the passionate desire to share, to give his experiences to others. Writing, passport to vision, is also passport to communication. That is why no writer can give it up. In so far as he seeks to communicate, and works at his instrument for that purpose, sharpening, refining, perfecting it, he is also equipping himself to receive the communication of other writers. He is their best reader. He knows the language. True, it may be urged that, in the given case, everyone knows it. Writing has, in fact, the disadvantages as well as the advantages belonging to a medium or tool in common employment, familiar to everybody. Many who would hesitate to criticize music or painting, on the ground that they are unfamiliar with their technique, criticize writing with freedom and aplomb, feel that they know all there is to know about it. They write letters: they talk: they are familiar with 'life'; it is enough. It is, as a matter of fact, by no means enough. The writer's reading of the books of others is wholly different from that of the 'plain man.' He reads, not word by word or paragraph by paragraph, but with steady eye to the shaping of the whole to expressive purpose; he can appreciate, as the other cannot, the form, the organization of the book, which makes it a book, instead of leaving it, in Flaubert's phrase, *'mille beaux endroits: pas un oeuvre.'* He gets more out of books than can any non-professional; gets what they get plus something they do not get.

How, then, should he give up the absorbing effort to express, to see, and to communicate? Of course he neither can nor will do so. His pains and penalties are his own; them, no reader is compelled to share. What that reader is offered — and, if he be a writer, can fully take — is a glimpse — it may be no more — of pattern in the universe, and a sense, more vivid than often comes in direct personal intercourse, of what sharing can be, and what communication. His expressive power, his faculty for communicating, may be faltering and imperfect. He hears the voices of angels and stutters in his report of them. That is a pity. It cannot be helped. He must continue to listen, since listening is for him life, must continue to try to record what he hears, since in that effort he gains knowledge of the fact that the voices are there. He possesses, and cannot part with, two things of intrinsic worth — a certainty of the inexhaustible possibilities inherent in his material, and a vision of the wonder, the significance, the beauty, and the order which that material for him registers and, for others, may reveal.

THE OLD FARMER'S ALMANAC

When all without is bleak and drear,
Within the humble cot
Choice books and conversation cheer;
Though many prize them not.
The cultured mind, with virtue's shield,
To lures of vice will seldom yield.
                              1842

JEANETTE EATON *supports Kenneth Grahame's dictum: 'Children are not merely people, they are the only living people we have left to us.'*

OUR MOST EXACTING AUDIENCE

NOT long ago when I was chatting with a distinguished critic a name was mentioned which sounded familiar. 'He's a writer, isn't he?' I inquired.

'Oh, well,' was the reply, uttered in a disparaging tone, 'he's done some *juvenile* books.'

The instant the words were sounded, realization of the likely wound to my feelings caused the critical eyes to widen with horror. But I only laughed. 'Never mind,' I said; 'doubtless writing books for young people doesn't make a real author, but it's a deeply rewarding vocation all the same.'

Condescension toward that vocation expressed by the critic takes many forms. Perhaps something in me draws it out. But certainly for years I have been accumulating direct evidence that this particular job of writing is often misapprehended. There is a widespread belief that somehow it should be based on the sort of technique which underlies the profession of teaching. I have been advised to teach a class of children in order to learn the principles of pedagogy. I have been urged to visit schools and to delve into the vocabulary studies which present an exact list of the words familiar to various age groups. The fact that I neither have children of my own nor any obvious association with them inspires the almost resentful challenge, often presented in a mere look, 'What makes you think you know anything about children, anyway?'

Now perhaps there are many successful and delightful authors for juniors who actually tread such suggested paths to the youthful heart. But my stubborn feet refuse to budge. I shed this deluge of advice so completely that no word of it dampens my spirits. Yet I may say I welcome this opportunity to state once and for all my feeling about my own approach to writing for boys and girls.

Yes, I say feeling. For I have no theories myself and run from them as a cat fishing in a lake scampers back from a high wave. It seems to me that psychological studies and external information about youthful mentality are quite inimical to the flow of imagination. The only difference between writing for adults and writing for youth is that one's capacity for imaginative projection must focus on the audience as well as on the subject matter. One has to be on both sides of the footlights at once. If I cannot *be* a child or that youngest adult whom we label adolescent when I write for either, then there's no use my putting pen to paper. For that is as much a part of the enterprise as the creation of character or the assemblage of facts. Were I to proceed within the fixed limits of a conscious theory, I'd not only produce a lifeless piece of work, but would probably commit that worst of all crimes — writing down for children.

Doubtless this is only an individual basis of work, not a universal law. Yet such autobiographies as Selma Lägerloff's and Jane Addams's and W. H. Hudson's 'Far Away and Long

Ago' seem to bear me out. Those books were written for adults. Yet so intensely do the authors relive their own youthful past that they have a profound appeal to junior readers.

It seems indisputable that adoption of an unsophisticated psychology is imperative, regardless of what is written for boys and girls. Somehow one must nibble the right side of the mushroom and swallow no more and no less than just the right amount. Then one attains the proper size for admission into the Wonderland of Youth. It is by no means altogether a dreamworld nowadays. But its landscape is not cluttered up with millions of impressions. Moreover, living things have not yet been uprooted by the ruthless analyst bent on his monstrous task of discovering through a microscope just how a mystery is working.

Whatever ingredients of that magic mushroom, it acts like a powerful herb. It makes the heart beat quicker and brings out a perfect rash of all the honesty within the system. At the same time, it purges away whatever is not sound and simple and charged with vitality. Neither the bluffers nor the disillusioned would be allowed to stay long in Wonderland. The cry, 'Off with their heads!' would ring from a million lusty throats and back would go these intruders to the adult realm where they belong.

Story books, fact books, nature books — all must have a kind of pellucid integrity to succeed with children. Had Kipling not felt the life of the jungle deeply and truly, he could have conjured up no magic. When Chief Standing Bear tells stories of the Sioux, Allan Villiers the adventure of whaling, and Christine Govan the tale of 'Those Plummer Children,' the audience knows that each in his own utterly different way is dealing with stuff intimately known and faithfully presented.

If Edwin Hamilton could not himself make a toy airplane which flew, he would certainly never dare face in print his horde of youthful followers.

It is true that boys and girls between the ages of fourteen and twenty are many times more mature today than they were a generation ago. But that is a mere matter of enlarged experience in a world which is very different from the world of thirty years past. Youth in any era is possessed of certain forces, spiritual forces, too strong to be easily turned aside. Inevitably that vital stream is focused on whatever comes its way, testing its truth. Not a logical, but an instinctive process, this. Consequently, although modern youth may be able to enjoy subtleties of humor and complications of motive, its hatred of bunk and sentimentality is keener than ever it was.

What teacher even in the jazz age would deny that a class of youngsters knows in a minute whether the instructor is master of his subject? How often do we hear from those who work constantly with young people that their judgment of individuals and of crucial situations is usually fair! This passion for sincerity is a more potent check on intellectualism in youth than it usually is — alas! — ever again. It enables boys and girls to respond in a living way to beauty and to some revelation of the mysteries of existence which mentally they may not quite understand. Doubtless some such idea of them as this made Kenneth Grahame, that matchless friend of dreamers, say, 'Children are not merely people, they are the only living people we have left to us.'

In presenting this argument, I am under no illusion about the horror of our times. Who, if not a person who writes biography, appreciates to the full the effect of the bad features of screen, radio, and newspaper? Great heroes of the past must compete for youthful attention with glorious gangsters, with impossible adventures of the comic strip, and the skit which comes over the air. But, at least, the situation contains a tremendous challenge to the competitor. One has the chance to prove that truth is stranger than fiction and equally exciting. One is impelled to wring every drop of drama from an age gone by and set a fast pace for the movement of one's tale.

Nowhere does a biographer feel this pressure more strongly than in the choice of that detail which will make another period come true. It is absolutely essential that characters of history be seen in their own setting of authentic costume, period furniture, and characteristic architecture. Manners, speech, and customs must be faithful to the times and the writer may serve up only such food and drink as a bygone menu provides. Yet nothing could be worse than stuffing one's pages like an antique shop.

Isn't it probably the weight of long descriptions which has borne Sir Walter Scott beneath the waters of neglect? And by the same token it is the instinctively right selection of whatever concisely conveys the look and feel of a past era which gives charm and authority to the books of Cornelia Meigs, Rachel Field, and Marquis James.

How well I remember my own struggle in writing 'Young Lafayette' to keep only the salient features of all the detail become so dear to me. The carving of Colonial doorways, the delightful minutiae of sword handles and snuffboxes, the enchanting trifles in drawing-room and kitchen! Hardest of all was to give up the big silver watch which had to be wound with a key.

That object, so eloquent of an age gone forever, has inherent amusement for a child of today. Yet in no natural fashion could it be got into my story. My impetuous young Marquis, to whom time was no object, simply would not stand still long enough to wind his watch for me. Apparently I had to choose between letting my narrative flow along its own course or deliberately halt it long enough to curve about the old timepiece. Therefore, I mournfully cast the watch after all the other alluring things I had thrown in the discard. It seems to me now that this was a triumph on the part of the youngster I had to be over the adult I am. For, after all, to a fifteen-year-old, the tale's the thing.

Such an instance explains why biography for the young is such a taxing affair. So many facts, carefully unearthed, piously checked, have to be thrown aside at the dictate of that other self. Just for the sake of a few paragraphs in 'A Daughter of the Seine' and in 'Young Lafayette,' I had to take many trips out to Versailles and there spend hours poking about the great palace and the gardens, gazing at old brown châteaux, observing all the mementoes of that mad, luxurious, glamorous period when Marie Antoinette so gaily piled the last straws on the humped back of France.

From such personal experience I can guess what great platters of American data were prepared by Constance Rourke in order to serve up the telling bits which give life to her book on Davy Crockett. As for those inimitable thumbnail sketches in the Benéts' 'A Book of Americans,' only someone concerned with the same problem can altogether value their peculiar flavor of rightness, achieved by a rare combination of scholarship and artistry.

Most of the names which appear on the shelves of the children's department are also emblazoned in the library proper. In other words, with a few exceptions like myself, my friend the critic would classify them as real authors. And yet, who knows, perhaps it is for the joy they bring to boys and girls that these same writers will live and flourish.

Here it is interesting to stop and ask ourselves why in such an age as this such a book as 'Little Women' should hold sway. One can hardly see what means of communication exist between present-day girls, with their idols of the 'Talkies,' their sports, their face-powder, their dancing-schools — all at fourteen years of age — and those utterly different creatures, Beth, Jo, and Amy. Yet because Miss Alcott drew the sap for her stories from her very own roots, she was able to produce a literary plant vigorous enough to grow even in a hothouse atmosphere.

For the same reason, quite as much as for fascinatingly unexpected turns of plot, 'Huckleberry Finn' and 'Tom Sawyer' are likely to remain deathless even though all the rest of their creator's works should perish from the earth. In this connection something very pertinent has been said by Eliza Orne White who could certainly never be left out of any discussion of juvenile literature. Now in her seventy-eighth year, this youthful writer says: 'I am able to remember vividly just how I felt when I was a child. The good thing about an imagination is that it defies time and bridges the gap between childhood and what, to the uninitiated, seems like an age.'

An explanation which only appears to be different from this accounts for the continued popularity of certain other classics. Take 'Treasure Island,' for example. The author of it, a delicate boy, grew up living so intensely in the world of daring imagination that it became far more real to him than is the scene of actual events to the average robust youth. Stevenson merely had to open the gate to his private domain and into it, with their instinctive flair for the real thing, rushed 'the people.' Until they lose that flair, children will keep on making straight between those same gateposts.

Similarly, the Quaker, Howard Pyle, living in his quiet Wilmington, could not be himself as a mere denizen of a sedate community. He had to contrive a land of thrilling adventure where his wild spirit roamed at will. As an adult with pen and brush in hand, he returned to that magic region and forked up 'Men of Iron' to satisfy fellow gallants of succeeding generations. These writers, and others like them, also went back to their roots quite as much as did Alcott and Mark Twain. Not to the geographical localities and external experiences of childhood days, but to the home soil of fancy which nourished their emotional existence. For Verity — thank the Eternal Powers — can don many a different guise!

Suppose you inquire of all those folk today who write for both juniors and adults whether they would willingly relinquish the youthful audience. I'll wager a postage stamp — which is all my vocation permits me to gamble — that not one among them would say yes. Whoever reported otherwise would be far gone in commercialism. For if these young tyrants keep us poor, they certainly make us honest.

SAMUEL JOHNSON

No man but a blockhead ever wrote except for money.

SAMUEL BUTLER

As soon as any art is pursued with a view to money, then farewell, in ninety-nine cases out of a hundred, all hope of genuine good work.

GEORGE BERNARD SHAW

You must not suppose, because I am a man of letters, that I never tried to earn an honest living.

DISRAELI

The author who speaks about his own books is almost as bad as the mother who talks about her own children.

BENJAMIN FRANKLIN

Nothing gives an author so much pleasure as to find his works respectfully quoted by other learned authors.

OLIVER WENDELL HOLMES

I never saw an author in my life, saving perhaps one, that did not purr as audibly as a full-grown domestic cat on having his fur smoothed the right way by a skillful hand.

> HAROLD NICOLSON *sees us as straws upon a stream: some interesting, some uninteresting. His passion for biography arises from a desire to examine that difference.*

HOW I WRITE BIOGRAPHY

I HAVE been invited to describe my personal experience of biography. I have been asked, more specifically, to divulge those influences which determined my choice of subject, sources, and material; to explain the methods by which I worked; and to discuss how the ensuing book corresponded to my own view of history and to my general philosophy of life. It was suggested at the same time that I should take one particular book as an illustration of my argument. What was required was not an article upon the general principles of biography so much as a confession of my own practice and experience in that ungentle art. I shall respond to that invitation as obediently as I can.

My first difficulty is that my biographical work has been of different kinds. I confess, indeed, that I have never written a 'pure' biography, in the sense that I have never written the life of an individual conceived solely as a work of art. I have thus written studies of Verlaine, Tennyson, and Swinburne which, although they contained much biographical material, were in fact attempts at literary criticism. My 'Byron: The Last Journey,' although more strictly biographical than the three books above mentioned, dealt only with the last twelve months of the poet's lifetime. 'Some People' was an experiment in the most impure form of biography, namely, that of biographical fiction. And in my other books, such as 'Portrait of a Diplomatist' and my more recent 'Curzon: The Last Phase,' my aim has been, not merely to paint the portrait of an individual, but also to record more than half a century of diplomatic history.

The above explanation, egoistic though it may seem, is essential to what follows. One day I hope to write a 'pure' biography and to concentrate upon describing the life and character of an individual from every angle and with no purpose other than such a description. As yet, however, I have never written a 'pure' biography and am therefore but an ill-bred specimen of the biographer. It is with full consciousness of my mongrel origin that I write these confessions.

What, to begin with, really *is* biography? It is the history of the life of an individual written as a branch of literature. As a history, it must be true. In that it describes an individual, it must be personal. And in that it is a branch of literature, it must be written with due regard to construction, balance, and style. The purely literary aspect is a question of personal temperament and taste. The problems of 'truth' and 'personality' are, however, the first two problems that the biographer has to face. As problems, they are far more difficult than they seem.

A biographer, for instance, is obliged, if he has any artistic conscience, to tell the truth and nothing but the truth. Is he also obliged to tell the *whole* truth? It is obviously impossible for one person to tell the whole truth about another person, even if they have been intimately acquainted for several years. This particular problem does not, however, present itself to the biographer in its general aspect; it presents itself in the form of a concrete instance. In my researches, for instance, into the last year of Byron's life I came across certain documents which threw a wholly new light, not only upon Byron's character, but even upon the problem of his separation and departure from England. To have divulged this information would have created a sensation and have destroyed for many romantic people the picture they had formed of Byron's character. I decided that I should make no use of this material except in so far as it colored and confirmed my own estimate of Byron's strangely complicated temperament. I think I was right in so doing, and I should justify my action upon the following biographical principle, listed under the heading of 'Truth and the Whole Truth.' My principle is as follows: 'If a biographer discovers material which is so sensational and shocking that it will disturb, not only the average reader, but the whole proportions of his own work, then he is justified in suppressing the actual facts. He is not justified, however, in suppressing the conclusions which he himself draws from those facts, and he must alter his portrait so that it conforms to those facts.' That is what I did in my treatment of Byron. Should some future research-worker come upon that same material he will recognize from my book that I also was in possession of that material, that it colored my interpretation of Byron's temperament, but that I suppressed the material itself for perfectly legitimate reasons.

The problem of 'personality' again, while it is akin to the problem of 'the whole truth,' takes devious forms. A biographer, if he is to achieve a coherent portrait, is obliged to select certain qualities or defects in his subject to which he gives especial emphasis. If he be an honest biographer he will be scrupulously careful to secure that this selection, or emphasis, is no distortion of the original. Yet not always will he find it easy to decide. A problem of this nature assailed me in my recent study of Lord Curzon. Curzon was notoriously selfish in money matters, and there were occasions when he behaved, in matters of personal property, in a manner unworthy of a gentleman. I was perplexed as to how to handle this element in his character. Knowing him intimately, I was aware that it represented only one of his many eccentricities. Yet I was also aware that those who had not known him intimately would see the whole picture in a false proportion. I thus merely alluded to his marked acquisitive instincts and gave no illustrations of the extent to which those instincts were manifested in his daily life. Here again I claim that I was justified. It was not that I desired to whitewash Curzon; it was merely that I knew that this eccentric failing would upset the proportions of my portrait and thereby convey an actually false impression. In principle, it is a mistake to suppress any weaknesses in one's subject. But in practice the honest biographer will find that the cause of truth is better served by the suppression of details which are disconcerting to the reader and which would falsify the ultimate impression left upon his mind.

I have begun my confessions with these two problems of truth and personality since they form a necessary introduction to the first item in the examination set me, namely, 'choice of subject.' In many cases, of course, the subject of a biography is imposed by adventitious circumstances. I was induced to write a biography of my father, published in the United States under the title of 'Portrait of a Diplomatist,' by obvious external considerations. When I had completed the book I was urged by friends to continue the thread of diplomatic history which it contained, and this led naturally to the second and third volumes of my trilogy on diplomatic history, namely, 'Peacemaking, 1919' and 'Curzon: The Last Phase.' In these three books, therefore, I did not, technically, 'choose my subject.' My study of Swinburne, also, was suggested to me from outside, and it may be for that reason that it is the worst book I have ever written. In regard to Verlaine, Tennyson, and Byron I did, however, 'choose my subject,' and I ought to be able to describe the motives which prompted this selection.

I remember well the genesis of my book on Verlaine, which was the first book I ever wrote. The Paris Peace Conference was drawing to its close, and one afternoon I walked back with Michael Sadleir from the Quai d'Orsay. 'I suppose,' I said to him, 'that it will all be rather flat when this is over. I have got so used to being overworked. What shall I do with the leisure which will follow?' 'You must write a book,' he answered. The idea struck me as highly original. It happened that on the few occasions when I had managed to get away from the work of the Conference I had amused myself by visiting the sites which Verlaine had frequented, having for years been fascinated by the life and poetry of that eccentric genius. Inevitably the name of Verlaine suggested itself to me, and from that moment I began to accumulate more detailed material. Tennyson, in his turn, was suggested to me, mainly by the fact that I had always appreciated his poetry, but also by my irritation at finding that so few of my contemporaries had ever tried to read or understand the work of the greatest of our English Laureates. My aim was, as I stated, to 'cut out the dead wood' from the dusty mass of the Tennysonian laurel clump, and to draw attention to his lyrical genius and to the true nature of his character. To Byron I was attracted, not only by personal sympathy, not merely by my own love of Greece, but also by the fact that the centenary of his death was rapidly approaching. Such, in so far as I can judge, were the motives which propelled me.

Yet if one is to say anything useful about this 'choice of subject,' mention must be made, not merely of the subjects chosen, but above all of those rejected. For several months, for instance, I accumulated material and wasted heavy hours in a desire to write a biography of Pope. I abandoned the project since I found, as I came to know Pope more intimately, that he was, as a character, profoundly distasteful to me. There were but few points of sympathetic contact. On another occasion I started upon a biography of Anselm. Here again I abandoned the attempt, yet on this occasion it was not incompatibility of temper that deterred me, but lack of adequate knowledge. I realized that my ignorance of scholasticism rendered it impossible for me to write a life of any eleventh-century Archbishop. A similar lack of topical knowledge prevented me from embarking recently upon a life of Benjamin Jowett — a man with whom I had many contacts but not that essential one with the religious temperament of 1858.

What, therefore, has all this to do with choice of subject, with 'truth' and 'personality'? It has this to do. The biographer may decide on his subject either from personal predilection or owing to external circumstances. He will at once be brought up against the problems of 'the whole truth' and 'unpleasant sides of personality.' Should he feel personally hostile, or unsympathetic, to his subject he will not resolve these problems in terms of a work of art. The distaste which he feels for his subject may not cause him to violate the canons of truth and personality, but it will certainly induce him to violate the canons of art. He will incline, that is, to prefer the sensational to the integral. My rule, therefore, upon this vital question of choice of subject is 'Never write a biography about anyone whom you personally dislike or from whose mental and topical atmosphere you are sundered either by prejudice or lack of knowledge.'

Having chosen a congenial subject, the next step is one of study or research. It is a question of method. My own method is invariable. First, I buy an enormous notebook strongly bound. Secondly, I obtain from the library, or purchase for myself, the most comprehensive textbook upon my subject which I can find. I then number the pages of my notebook and prepare an index at the beginning. I then take the dates of birth and death of my hero and write out a table at the end showing exactly what age he had reached in any given year. Having done this, I start to summarize my textbook. The first page will be headed 'heredity,' the third 'parents and childhood,' the fifth 'school and early influences,' and so on throughout the man's career. On page 50 or so of the notebook will start the sections on character, which in their turn will be carefully indexed. Thus, page 50 might be headed 'epileptic tendency,' page 51 'ambition,' page 53 'selfishness,' page 55 'sense of humor, lack of,' and so on. All entries from the main textbook must be made in black ink: the right-hand page is folded in half, leaving the left-hand page a blank. By the time the main textbook has been annotated in this manner, the majority of the right-hand pages will be filled if not with material, then at least with headings. The temptation to shirk these notes by taking them in the form of references must strongly be resisted. It is a mistake, for instance, to write on page 73 of one's notebook 'for good story about his drinking see Havelock, Vol. II, page 353.' Conversely, it is also a mistake to omit references which may be required later. The Havelock story must be summarized in your notebook and the salient passages quoted in inverted commas. At the end of the passage must appear the reference 'Havelock, Vol. II, page 353.' Only by such industrious methods can the material be properly digested, since, when, at a later stage, you begin actually to write the book, a mere reference will convey nothing to you, whereas to have to look up that reference a second time is a duplication of labor. Your main notebook must contain all the undigested material of the final work: it must not contain mere references to pages in other books.

Having read the main textbook, you must then purchase or acquire all the other books on the subject. According as you read these, you must insert the passages you may require to use on the right hand page of your notebook. If you have folded that page in half you will be able to insert the additional information exactly opposite the relevant passage from the main textbook. Having read all the published works upon your subject you then enter a further stage — that of original research.

If you are writing a biography of someone long dead this will be a delightful and impersonal labor. But if you are dealing with a man whose friends and relations are still alive you will be involved in difficulties. On the one hand is the desire to obtain hitherto unpublished material. On the other hand there is the conflict which will arise between 'personal obligation' and truth. Let me define what I mean by 'personal obligation.' When writing my book on Tennyson, for instance, I was offered the opportunity of obtaining from Tennyson's son many unpublished papers. Knowing the religious veneration which the second Lord Tennyson retained for the memory of his father I rejected this opportunity. I was aware, in the second place, that were I to accept such material I should be placing myself under a 'personal obligation' to the family of the deceased and would in common decency be precluded from saying anything which might cause them pain. I solemnly warn the intending biographer against this common danger of his profession.

Another danger of research in the biography of the recently dead is the unreliability of human evidence. Much of one's information must of necessity be derived from oral evidence. Such evidence is often confidential and seldom trustworthy. When the book is published, other people write to the press accusing you of inaccuracy. Your only reply is to quote your authorities, who all too often refuse to be quoted. All oral evidence, even when it comes from your subject himself, must if possible be checked by reference to others.

Having completed your notebook, having read all published books and gathered all available evidence, the next thing to do is to take a short holiday. That holiday must be spent in visiting the localities identified with the subject of your biography. This delightful pilgrimage must always be deferred until the last moment. Only after you have amassed all possible information it is profitable to visit the scene of your drama. Any premature visit leads to subsequent regret. If you have journeyed prematurely from Cleveland to Aberdeen, it is irksome, on returning to Ohio, to come across a book which gives you a whole new aspect of the Aberdeen period. No biography should ever be written unless the author has personally visited the places he describes; yet no biographer should visit these places until he has read and digested all possible material. His journey should be the breathing-space between the period of research and the period of writing.

On his return from this pilgrimage the biographer should settle down to his book. His first act will be to reread his notebook (which by that date should be a bulging portmanteau containing endless loose leaves inserted in their proper place and secured by a huge external band) and to block out the headings of his several chapters. He then starts to write — and from that moment I have no further advice to give him.

Such have been the methods which I have invariably followed. There is one question which remains. 'How far,' they ask me, 'do your own books correspond to your philosophy of life and your view of history?' That is a question which it is impossible to answer. I should be much distressed were I to feel that my philosophy of life had become rigid and recognizable. That would indeed imply the arterio-sclerosis of later middle age. I should hesitate even to claim for myself a rigid view of history. Perhaps this very fluidity of conviction implies an attitude towards life, or at least a state of mind. If there be any recurrent thesis in my biographical work I suppose it is this: 'Human error is a constant, and not an incidental, factor in history. Everybody is an ass sometimes, and most people are asses all the time. Human will power is an intermittent factor, and history has been made more frequently at moments when people had no idea what they wanted than at those rarer moments when some individual wanted something definite. We are all straws upon the stream: yet if one observes those straws they do not all behave in exactly the same manner.' Were I to define my philosophy of history I should, I suppose, define it in some such terms.

'But what,' you will say, 'is the stream?' And to that I answer: 'I have no idea whatsoever; I know only that it is there. And the more interesting straws behave in a manner different from that adopted by the less interesting straws. My passion for biography arises from a desire to examine that difference.'

BURTON RASCOE

What no wife of a writer can ever understand, no matter if she lives with him for twenty years, is that a writer is working when he is staring out of the window.

KATHLEEN NORRIS

The reason why people like my books is that I write of life as I want it to be.

LENIN

Every book must help our proletarian movement, must be a cog in the social mechanism of our united working class.

PEARL S. BUCK

Never, if you can possibly help it, write a novel. It is a thoroughly unsocial act.

LA BRUYÈRE

It is the glory and merit of some men to write well, and of others not to write at all.

RAINER MARIA RILKE

This above all: ask yourself in the stillest hour of the night: must I write?

VALENTINE WILLIAMS
detects a certain affinity between a Rolls-Royce, a dress coat from Savile Row, and the perfectly constructed mystery story.

ON CRIME FICTION

I DON'T know whether novelists have a private patron saint — so many of us do our own patronizing, don't we? — but Saint François de Sales has been adopted as the protector of writers in general and to that holy man I sometimes put up a prayer. 'You can have your dialogue,' I say to him, speaking familiarly as to a colleague, 'and you can have your plots. Grant me only the gift of construction!'

Your tired business man, commonly referred to by the craft, in this alphabetical age, as the T.B.M., who grabs an armful of thrillers at the news-stand and leaves them in the train, may not realize that the secret of the good shocker lies, first and last, in its architecture. You may take it from me that I know. From my childhood days I have saturated myself in this branch of fiction, from the 'Memoirs of Vidocq,' father of an enormous progeny of detective stories, to 'The House of the Whispering Pines,' from 'Monsieur Lecoq' to 'The Nebuli Coat,' and the experience I have acquired in perpetrating thrillers myself fills me with a sort of despairing admiration for the brilliant construction which has commanded success for the classic examples of the *genre*.

Many modern disciples of Dumas and Poe, of Stevenson and Conan Doyle, have the gift of lively dialogue. More possess the knack of stringing together a chain of hair-raising adventures. But how many are capable of turning out a well-tailored story, one of those yarns as snugly fitting as a Savile Row dress coat, with a plot that neither bags nor sags nor wrinkles, a supremely skilful blend of romance, mystery, humour, suspense, and surprise? How hard to light upon the combination in contemporary fiction, yet, when found, how easily and rapturously is it recognized!

Every shocker-enthusiast will know what I mean. I need not cite 'The Moonstone,' 'The Murders in the Rue Morgue,' Gaboriau's all but forgotten little masterpiece, 'Le Petit Vieux des Batignolles,' or, to come down to our own day, my friend E. C. Bentley's solitary and dazzling contribution to this form of novel in 'Trent's Last Case,' as instances of plots so adroitly turned that in their dénouements every piece slides into place as smoothly as the cogs of a Rolls-Royce changing gear. And the proof is that what remains in the reader's mind is not the memory of this or that character but the gist of the plot — the man who stole the moonstone in his sleep, the murder committed by an orang-utang. Which is as much as to say that the author has achieved plausibility, the most important as it is the most difficult part of his task.

Plausibility is the first essential in a craft which relies almost wholly upon technique. Crime fiction is by no means easy to write; there is no form of fiction to which the old saw that 'Hard writing makes easy reading' more truthfully applies, for the secret of success depends upon construction. There are many novels in which a talent for characterization and dialogue compensates for faulty construction. But not in the detective story.

The characters may be wooden (they often are), psychology a missing quantity; but the mechanism must be well-greased, however much the personages creak at the joints as the author pushes them in and out of his plot.

Plausibility's the thing, my masters. It doesn't matter very much what it is you want the reader to believe — the important aim is to make him believe it. I like the tale about the great Duke of Wellington who at a large garden party was accosted by a polite stranger who, lifting his hat, said, 'Mr. Ramsbotham, I believe?' To which the Duke, at that time probably the best-known figure on the European scene, replied genially, 'My dear sir, if you believe that, you'll believe anything!' That's the quality — the quality of believing anything — the crime-fiction author would like to find in his reader.

Unfortunately, it is not so easy as that. Implicit belief can be secured only by cultivating plausibility. Alexandre Dumas *père*, who knew something about it, gave us his recipe. 'Be plausible in your first chapter or two,' he said, 'and your reader will swallow anything thereafter.' But plausibility, which means fidelity to life, premises in the writer a mind highly critical of his own work and as prompt to reject the impossible situation as to eschew the danger of dislocating the long arm of coincidence. Some contend that plausibility does not matter so long as the tale be exciting. That won't wash — at any rate, not with the detective story writer who knows his job.

The lay-out of the crime must be credible or, at least, characters and background so credibly depicted that they outweigh any inherent improbabilities of plot. The argument that extraordinary situations and staggering coincidences are the commonplaces of real life won't do. Truth is stranger than fiction, but fiction simply cannot afford to be as improbable as real life. The writer of a thriller is not allowed to say to himself, 'This remarkable set of circumstances has actually occurred, therefore, I am justified in using them for my plot.' It may happen to a man that a pipe bursts in the bathroom and his mother-in-law has a fit on the same morning; but a playwright who should use these devices for getting his characters off the stage would be laughed at as a bungling amateur. The crime-fiction author has to spin his web strictly within the framework of what may be called the common denominator of human events and he may not go outside it unless prepared to take a lot of trouble to build up for and justify the excursion. Incidentally, this appears to me to be a valid argument against the present-day tendency to base detective stories on actual crime cases.

Highbrows who, nevertheless, read us with such avidity, are apt to speak pityingly of shockers as 'that sort of thing.' I wonder if they realize what desperate hard work the technique of 'that sort of thing' imposes upon the unfortunate craftsman. Tempo, for example, one of the most difficult aspects of the case. A detective story must move. The crime may be deliberate, but never the story. There are no laurels awaiting the most leisurely murder yarn on record any more than there were jobs forthcoming for the two men who presented themselves to the great Barnum as the shortest giant and the tallest dwarf in the world.

The author has to get off the mark quickly and keep moving from situation to situation and from disclosure to disclosure. No half-dozen chapters for him as a sort of desultory first act for the introduction of characters and motif: no pleasant dawdling about the hero's or the heroine's early days on the farm, no pen pictures of dawn over the moors or sunset on the lake at

Topsail Towers. He has to start — literally, very often — with a bang and trust to his skill to slip into the breathless, crowded events of his opening the indispensable presentation of characters, environment and theme. On more than one occasion, I have rewritten the opening chapters of a mystery story three or four times until satisfied that the action did not flag; again and again I have transposed the order of chapters with the same intent. For the self-respecting novelist this branch of fiction is one long fight between a relentless technique on the one hand and, on the other, his natural instinct to depict his characters as they appear and illuminate the fountain springs of their actions.

Take the matter of the harmless but necessary corpse. You can open with the discovery of the murder and proceed to develop the victim's personality and environment by means of that now somewhat discredited device, the switch-back; or you can achieve the same end, piecemeal, in the course of the subsequent investigation. My preference, as far as my stories are concerned, is for presenting the victim alive, delaying demise for a chapter or two, as I have a feeling that the average reader is apt to be more interested in a crime when the victim is someone he has known before he became a 'stiff.' A famous critic — I think it was the late Alan Dale — once said that he never bothered to see the first act of a play because anyone can write a first act. In the same way, it is not difficult to devise a swift and gripping opening to a detective story by planting a dead body in Chapter One — where the skill comes in is in showing how it got there and in introducing the different *dramatis personae* without slowing down the pace.

Another standing problem is the question of who is going to elucidate the crime. If plausibility is the author's god, as it should be, he will recollect that in real life dead bodies are really not left about, cluttering up the house. When someone is murdered, people have an inveterate habit of calling in the police. Detective fiction has produced a respectable crop of official investigators who even, on occasion, provide the love interest as well. The average detective inspector, however, if realistically depicted is scarcely of the stuff of which fictional heroes are made — for this the bureaucratic mind is far too literal; and as far as the love interest goes, the hard-boiled cop from Scotland Yard or Center Street can scarcely be considered a promising target for Cupid's darts. Crime fiction has overcome this snag by evolving the type of amateur criminologist.

The amateur criminologist enjoys many advantages. For one thing he is able to disregard those laws relating to the liberty of the subject which so grievously hamper the police; he has no official hierarchy over him to restrict his freedom of action; or need he give thought to such mundane matters as expense accounts in pursuing his investigations. Although many crime fiction addicts, I believe, regard a love interest as entirely superfluous, the amateur criminologist at least gives the author the chance to lighten what might be otherwise the unrelieved gloom of his tale by providing a nice and probably slightly misunderstood heroine to share the vicissitudes of the investigation.

And this brings me to what is probably the most delicate task of all and that is, the nice adjustment of the balance between the two investigators, the inevitable arm of the law and the amateur. Unless he is very careful, the author is likely to find two heroes on his hands instead of one — the professional who, for plausibility's sake, really has a certain function to fulfill if only to look foolish while the amateur teaches him his business, and the aforesaid amateur. In my experience the professional sleuth-hound is a considerable nuisance. He keeps drifting in and out of the story, slowing down the pace of the narrative, whenever he appears, with his interminable but alas! indispensable string of questions. I still derive a glow of satisfaction from the thought that in 'The Portcullis Room' I got rid of such intruders altogether by the simple device of having the castle in the Hebrides, where the crime takes place, cut off by a storm so that the police only arrive on the scene when all is over bar the wedding bells.

There is yet another angle of the detective-story writer's task calling for the mastery of considerable technique and that is in the matter of explanations — the how- and why-it-happened. The closing chapters are a deadly trap. The demon Anti-Climax hovers menacingly over them. Ah, those final chapters, with their wearisome, if conscientious, harking-back to details which the reader has probably forgotten but which cannot be overlooked if loose ends are to be neatly tied, all shipshape and Bristol fashion; their dying depositions, their handy suicides, all mixed up with the gloatings of the amateur over the professional investigator, hand-shakes, back-slappings, and last-line embraces! One of the tricks the writer has to acquire is the art of feeding explanations to the reader as the story progresses so that the closing stages shall not become a mere tangle of loose ends which have to be dealt with before the magic word FINIS can be written.

As one who has experimented with both categories of mystery fiction, adventure tales and straight detective stories, I consider that the standard of the former is higher, but the latter are more arduous to write. With its tangle of clues, real and false, crime fiction calls for the most rigid concentration and attention to detail and a turn of mind which is mathematical rather than imaginative. On the other hand in a detective story the elucidation of the crime to some extent exempts the author from the necessity for elaborate characterization. Indeed, the woodenness of the characters in many of the most successful crime stories suggests that, in this type of thriller, the play, rather than the players, is the thing.

Mystery stories of the adventure order make exacting demands upon the writer. He must exercise enormous restraint. The mystery must be dense, but not too complicated: the reader should be fogged but never bewildered; and the veil may not be lifted too soon. Most important of all, there must be a strong and plausible plot so that, when the mystery is dispersed, the underlying structure is found to be worth disclosing.

The majority of these stories centre about a sinister character, as in 'The Woman in White,' 'Dracula,' or 'The Beetle.' Here, too, the novelist must retain his sense of proportion, for an excess of villainy, even as a multiplicity of villains, verges upon the ludicrous. Personally, the celebrated Professor Moriarty, the master-mind of crime, always left me cold, possibly because Sherlock Holmes leaves no place for a second superman upon the canvas. The renown of that interminably spun-out tale 'The Woman in White' rests uniquely upon the character of the villain. In creating Count Fosco, with his birds and his mellow tenor voice, the practised hand of Wilkie Collins distributed the values so perfectly that the figure of the Count haunts the reader's mind long after the intricate plot has been forgotten. The trouble is that, as I have said, the standard of this type of story is high, all the way from those glowing opening chapters of 'Monte Cristo' to the strange ship in 'The Wrecker.' Today celebrated novelists, their fame already secure in other branches of their calling, have begun to try their hand at shockers, with a varied degree of success which suggests that the writing of thrillers is not quite so easy as it looks.

The present vogue of mystery fiction, especially crime fiction, is extraordinarily robust and shows no signs of diminishing. Indeed, if anything, it is on the increase — women, in particular, are challenging in growing numbers what used to be virtually a male monopoly in this respect. The craze has swept the civilized world and the novels of the leading exponents of the craft, especially those published in English, are nowadays translated into a dozen different foreign tongues, including Japanese.

The delight of human nature in a puzzle is age-old. The origins of crime fiction are lost in the sands of time. There are examples in the Bible — the story of Susannah and the Elders, for instance, and of the Prophet Daniel and King Astyages, in the Apocrypha. The Orient has always had a taste for crime fiction, as witness the Arabian Nights, and to this day, in the market-places of the East, the professional story-tellers hold their audiences rapt with the recital of classical examples, usually setting forth how some luckless wight, unjustly accused of a crime, exposed the real author by means of deductive processes of reasoning. In his opening to 'The Murders in the Rue Morgue,' Edgar Allan Poe, the father of detective fiction as we know it today, dwells upon this quality of the mind which exults in disentangling a problem. He had this kind of mind himself. Ciphers and anagrams were his hobby until he read the 'Memoirs of Vidocq' and thereafter applied his deductive and analytical powers, till then occupied with the deciphering of puzzles, to setting and solving of crime problems.

We are asked to believe that the intelligentsia resort to the crime novel as a form of escape from the stress of modern life. I should like to point out that this is the justification for dramatic literature generally, and also for the theatre. Detective fiction appeals to a certain tendency in human nature, it is agreed, but in my opinion the extraordinarily uneven level of the common run of novels published today is in no small measure responsible for the continued popularity of the detective story. There are plenty of rubbishy crime novels about; but while the indifferent detective story may bore the reader, it will rarely shock or disgust him as nowadays one of the so-called psychological novels picked at random is likely to do. There is blood in the crime story, but not dirt. And its difficult technique is in some sort a guarantee that a detective novel put out by a reputable publishing house, even though the author be comparatively unknown, will be reasonably good of its kind.

Certain unwritten laws preside over the relationship existing between the crime-fiction author and his public. The author must play fair with his reader. In the straightforward crime story the solution usually depends on the correct interpretation of one or more salient facts. Once they are correctly stated, the answer comes pat, like a sum in arithmetic. It is the author's right, indeed, his duty, to so obscure these facts as to delay the reading of the riddle up to the last possible moment. But the reader must feel that he and the investigator are starting from scratch. It shall be assumed, then, that the murderer is one of the characters mainly featured throughout the story: in other words, the author shall not be permitted to drag in the real culprit, more or less as an afterthought, in the later stages of the book.

Again, what the author states out of his own consciousness shall be true and accepted as such: that is to say, if he declares, *as author*, that the room in which the body is found is devoid of all means of egress except the door, he shall not be at liberty to contend later that the murderer escaped by the chimney. On the other hand, such a statement may be placed in the mouth of one of the characters with all propriety. The Detection Club of London, an organization of British detective-story writers, goes farther than this. Candidates for admission are required to swear a solemn oath that in their stories they will make no use of 'poisons unknown to science, death rays, bands of Chinamen, or the Act of God,' or words to that effect. On their side, readers of crime fiction have their obligations, too. They may not skip, or dip ahead to see who committed the murder, or — most heinous of all — shall they divulge to their families or friends the real identity of the criminal.

It may be that the present vogue of the mystery novel will pass, at least in its present acute form. But in my opinion there will always be a public for the well-constructed, swift-moving tale. Suspense: surprise: sufficient characterization to heighten the drama by making the characters behave like human beings: extreme plausibility and action, action, action — these, it is submitted, are the ingredients of which the successful mystery story is blended.

KATHERINE MANSFIELD

Major literature is, in short, an initiation into truth.

CHEKOV

The aim of fiction is absolute and honest truth.

JOSEPH CONRAD

Every novelist must begin by creating for himself a world, great or little, in which he can honestly believe.

TURGENEV

You must be remorselessly true to your sensations and emotions.

SOMERSET MAUGHAM

People accuse me of being cynical or bitter, whereas I am simply trying to set down my impressions of strange and ruthless forces that are beyond my control.

ERNEST HEMINGWAY

Good writing is architecture, not interior decoration.

PHYLLIS BOTTOME *decries optimism without courage, morals without reality, crimes without penalties, and wit without the weight of thought.*

THE RESPONSIBILITIES OF A WRITER

THE writer has perhaps no more responsibility than other human beings, but his responsibilities go further afield. The normal man confines his obligations to his home, his job and his community; but the writer's obligations are to a wider audience, and have to include the truth of his heart.

The first responsibility of a writer is to himself, as any man's is; and this is a fundamental responsibility which in the artist's case has a direct influence upon his audience.

No man can give what he has not got; and in the long run he will give what he has got, however much he may wish to disguise the shape of this involuntary generosity.

Goethe used to say: 'Do not tell me what a man thinks; nor what he says; I shall be none the wiser about him; but tell me what he does and I shall know him.'

Deception can be successfully practised for a long time, though it requires more skill and trouble than the truth, but the only permanently duped person is the deceiver's self.

A famous painter of animals in motion once said to me, 'I

daren't hang those cats of mine on the wall — they would be such an indecent self-exposure.'

The man who is not an artist escapes this predicament. He can keep his qualities in the back of his shop, whereas the artist has to put them in the front window. In the very act of creation, an artist reveals not only the object he is at work upon but the nature of the worker.

All artists, writers as well as painters, realize, however far they may put the subject from themselves, that what is in them becomes a part of what they are trying to express. Painters put themselves as well as their models into their portraits. The Pope in Velasquez's greatest portrait was a weak man whose mistress locked him up whenever she went out, for fear he might be tempted to give his money to her rivals, but Velasquez himself, with all his strength, looks out of those weak eyes down all the centuries. Novelists, however careful they may be not to draw the characters of their friends in their novels, never escape portraying themselves.

Henry James, who understood his job and its nature perhaps more thoroughly than any novelist before or since, once said to a writer friend who asked for his criticism of her work: 'If I may say so, you appear not to have cut the umbilical cord between your writing and yourself.' The child must bear a resemblance to its parents but it should have a separate existence.

This responsibility of self-portrayal forces upon the writer the necessity for being intellectually a 'full man.' If he has not filled his mind with the vital energy of first rate thinkers, how can he give his readers anything more solid than gas?

A writer who has not deeply, patiently and wisely read, is like a cook who relies solely on his sense of taste to produce culinary masterpieces.

Taste in books or cookery has to be formed, and the only way to form taste, is to study the best that has been produced by the best minds dealing with the subject.

Since a writer cannot make his own ego, it is his responsibility to face up to it. An honest writer does not try to be better or worse than he knows he is. An honest grocer keeps his sugar free from sand; and an honest writer keeps his imagination free from humbug. Whatever comes out of him is what has been inside him and it is part of his job to see that what is inside him — his thoughts, and the very stuff of his heart — is fit for the public to read. An artist's fitness lies in his integrity and he is moral or unmoral according to his intellectual truthfulness.

If he is not an honest man he had better change his profession for that of some more obscure type of manual worker, where his dishonesty is less likely to be found out and less injurious to the public if it is found out. The fate of an insincere writer is a twofold torment; the intelligent public finds him out and despises him, and he becomes accepted with rapture by a company of nitwits and humbugs whose favorite fantasies he is compelled to voice.

If an artist is honest, his work will be carried down to the roots of his being until it becomes an organic part of himself. What is called 'originality' in an artist — if it is rightly so called — is nothing but complete absence of duplicity.

We should all be original if we were truthful, for no man's truth is quite the same as another man's. What is the same is the method of trying to hide himself advantageously behind screens.

Adam and Eve started this method in the Garden of Eden, when finding after the Fall that they were naked, they hid from God, although their appearance could have given Him no great shock since He had created them in the first instance without clothes. A fiction writer has a great many screens to hide behind if he likes — or if he prefers to be a genuine artist, he has as many channels for revealing himself truthfully.

One has only to read the great writers of fiction to realize how completely and therefore originally they reveal themselves. We need no biography of Jane Austen, Dostoievsky or Flaubert. What they were they have already given us.

When William Wordsworth told Charles Lamb that he was persuaded he could write like Shakespeare if he had a mind to it, Charles Lamb replied, that he had always supposed it was the mind that was wanting.

The fiction writer has a responsibility beyond that to his own character, he must try to respect equally the character of his creations. They must have room to grow and the sort of soil that suits them to grow in. They must not be pressed into the service of his pet ideas, they must voice their own kind of thoughts and act not as the novelist pictures himself as acting but as they would picture themselves as acting were they the novelist.

A philosopher, a poet, or a critic has a right to exploit his favourite ideas in his work, but the novelist has no such right; he must voice the ideas which would be characteristic of his creatures. Only in the case of his choosing himself as the character through whose eyes the chief life of the book appears, dare he reveal his own pet fancies. His self-revelation, in his more objective characters, does not lie in the realm of the conscious, it is portrayed by his attitude to one and all of his creations.

He will reveal himself whether he wants to or not, but he will best reveal himself by the complete objectivity with which he reveals others.

In order to have a disinterested understanding from which to draw his characters, he must renew his own mind by thought and reading as well as by personal contacts; good criticism will help him, but unfortunately good criticism is rare and good critics are too often forced to slice up their minds, to meet the fearful mass of material thrust at them by editors and publishers.

A novelist can never afford to forget what William Hunt said of painting — 'It is the background that makes the bird.'

If the crops of an author's mind follow too quickly upon each other, they must inevitably impoverish the earth they spring from. Writers should be thinkers. Alfred Adler, the psychologist, says that a neurosis is the exploitation of a shock; in the same way, the imagination of an artist is the exploitation of experience; but just as the shock must be genuine to create a neurosis, so the experience must be genuine to awaken the imagination of the artist, and it comes to few minds, however lively, to have first-hand experience often enough to justify a continuous output.

It is no easy task to make food for thought. Heine said: 'Out of my great sorrows I have made little songs.'

Few writers can turn their experiences into the value of Heine's little songs, but their responsibility is the same — to give the true expression of their minds to the public.

If a writer gives the public shoddy material, flimsy emotions; cheap deductions, sentimental rather than real stories; 'wise cracks' rather than real wit; melodrama instead of drama, he has cheated his public and failed in at least two of his responsibilities — the responsibility to himself and the responsibility to his audience. The public may not always be aware of adulteration in a book or work of art until it has tried something better, just as the unwary buyer accepts the grocer's sanded sugar until he has found unsanded sugar with which to compare it. The buyer may even have a faulty palate and prefer bad sugar to good.

Many readers demand happy endings, optimism without courage; morals without reality; crimes without penalties; wit without the weight of thought, but they do so at their peril. They too have failed in their fundamental responsibility as human beings by seeking to escape truth, and Truth — that mighty Hunter before the Lord — will catch up with them sooner or later and pay them out for it.

Such writers and such readers are not the concern of a serious artist. He knows that whether the public likes it or not, whether he earns more or less money by it, he must speak and write the truth that is in him. It is his job, and if he fails to carry it out, he ceases to be a genuine artist and becomes instead a mere entertainer or what is much more injurious, a self-seeking charlatan.

An entertainer has his uses in the world. He relaxes strain and eases the tension of exhausted minds, but what he gains is only of momentary value, he cannot sustain the tired heart, or nerve the soul to fight better.

The entertainer cannot create life; and the artist if he is true to himself is always creating life. It is his business to pour the wine of his being into fresh forms.

The question of selling his thoughts should be the public's responsibility rather than the artist's. The artist has to live on something, and if his created imaginings are worth anything to other people, he has as much right to expect payment as a baker has to be paid for making bread.

The difference between the baker and the artist is that the

artist is more involved in his work. Even if the baker is a very good baker, there is less of him in his loaf of bread than there is of the artist in his work of art. Both should be skilled workmen and both supply the public with what it needs, but whereas the baker more or less mechanically supplies an immediate want, the artist, by his own growth and with himself as material, has to supply a less immediate want. He has even to train his audience to realise their need of his produce, whereas nature settles the need of the baker's audience. The artist's is therefore both a more arduous and a more precarious profession than the baker's, but it is probably a good deal more fun.

Unfortunately, readers are as a rule even less trained than writers, and since the recognition of truth does not always bring them ease, they are apt to jib at what is good for them. A trained reader knows that what a genuine artist gives him is fresh life.

He feels instantly — 'This writer respects me. He is giving me the best he has. He is a fellow man and has been touched by the spirit of my infirmities.' For no true artist is a 'highbrow' or a 'superior person.' He knows that his material is the same as any other man's; it is the use he makes of his material which proves him to be an artist.

The honest reader puts down a real book with a feeling of release and self-congratulation. He has contributed something to it himself — the quality of his attention was worth what it has been given. There should always be the power to release in a work of art, for every good artist is a doctor of the mind. It is a relief if he merely says 'your pain is there,' although he cannot always cure it. Pain can be beyond relief, as it is in the greatest tragedies of Shakespeare and Euripides; but the pity and strength called out in tragedy, match and support the reader's own experience. There is a bracing quality in high tragedy which nerves the reader to face life afresh; and to bear its personal griefs with a new courage.

It is worse than useless for a doctor to promise relief from all the ills that flesh is heir to, and he endangers the lives of his patients by false palliatives. Such a man is a menace to the public, and so is such a writer. To excite feelings that are foolish and unsound; to promise rosy futures and easy escapes where no such things are possible, is a great danger to the public mind. False coiners of emotion reduce the true currency of the human heart.

Many novels written with great skill and charm are wholly fallacious and morally perverting because they portray human beings who do not have to pay for their fun. There are no such human beings; and there is no such fun. Cheats may be attractive, but they are not honest men and should not be given that peculiar attraction of reliability which can only be found in honest people. Immoral women have the attraction of immorality, but not that of virtue — and virtuous women — alas — only too certainly have not the attraction of harlots. Physically, very pretty shams can be put on the market, but spiritually figs remain figs and thistles thistles.

The most rudimentary qualification for an artist is his intellectual sincerity. He can lie to others all day long if he wants to, so long as he knows he is doing it, but the moment he lies to himself by falsifying what he is portraying, he is no longer an artist. The sham Publican is the same as the sham Pharisee — their fallacy lies in thinking they are not as other men are. The artist knows he is what other men are and he has taken both time and pains, to find out the stuff of which all human beings are made.

An artist cannot afford pessimism or optimism, since both

these habits of mind are neurotic; it is his lot to keep an open mind and to face what comes along without prejudice. Browning tells the soul of man 'to greet the unseen with a cheer.' This is no doubt a courageous thing to do, but it is probably a more courageous, because more reasonable thing, to greet the unseen without cheering.

It is a fatal mistake for a writer to think too poorly of human nature, or to believe that cheap substitutes can permanently satisfy the mind of man.

The ignorant cease to be ignorant; the young grow up; the sentimental learn that nothing is interesting which is not true.

It is for the artist to show the public — after he has discovered it for himself — that there is such a thing as abstract truth. There is a definite standard for the mind set up by its truest exponents. Works of Art have characteristics by which real critics know them and can reveal them to others. This is the value of a critic. He is a midwife to genius, and on his knowledge of his profession, the safety of many lives depends. The critic should be a safeguard to the artist and he is very often merely a panderer to the bad taste of the public and a direct discouragement to the harried soul of the immature but promising artist; for artists are made, not born, and there is very little luck about anything.

It is hard enough for the artist, dependent as he is for his daily bread on the good will of his audience, not to let the failure of the moment tempt him away from his inner vision, or harder still, if his work has been accepted, not to run between the blinkers of the world's applause.

The critic should help to keep him from both these dangers. He should find out what the writer means and explain it to the public, and only if a writer means nothing should he unequivocally condemn. The question of unequivocally praising should not arise at all in a world of imperfect human beings.

The author must not let his public colour his views of fact; he must try to follow his own emotions without exaggeration. He is no trained nurse to put on a cheerful voice for the sick room nor need he lower everybody's temperature because he suffers from cold feet. If he expects the public to trust him — and in the long run they will trust him if he gives them grounds for it — he must also trust them.

Not all readers are tired business men, nor are all young girls so susceptible to evil that the facts of life must be juggled with in order to preserve their innocence. Most innocence can preserve itself and most tired business people can be rested by a genuine piece of work better than by a sham. There are victims, of course, but artists should pity rather than cater for these unfortunates. Civilization is responsible for them and the artist can best quicken civilization into self-improvement by appealing to what is best in it rather than by attempting to shield its victims.

It is one of the Alice in Wonderland portents of modern life (perhaps to be accounted for by the timidity of middlemen) that many audiences have better taste than might appear from the works of art presented to them. They are looking for bread and being presented with stones. Sooner or later they may get really hungry and as hunger is dangerous to middlemen — it is to be hoped that the middlemen will grow timid in the opposite direction and insist on producing the few best — rather than the many bad — novels which are cluttering up the stream of time. It is too much to expect that middlemen will give up being timid — but a hopeful mind may foresee a time when the middlemen themselves may be given up, and the creative artist be left face to face with an intelligent audience. Meanwhile nothing will alter the beneficent fact — that in the long run sand in the imagination does not pay; nor the ruthless one — that the writer's fundamental responsibility is to see that it never gets there.

SAMUEL ELIOT MORISON

Contemporary English and French historians have proved that history can be both sound and interesting. To restore this most human and noble branch of literature to its once high estate in our country, and to give our own history, with all its comedy and tragedy, its color and passion, the esteem it deserves, we must preserve all that the elders have taught us of historical method and reverence for truth; but we must also learn how to write English.

H. A. L. FISHER

Men wiser and more learned than I have discerned in history a plot, a rhythm, a predetermined pattern. These harmonies are concealed from me. I can see only one emergency following upon another, as wave follows wave, only one great fact with respect to which, since it is unique, there can be no generalizations, only one safe rule for the historian; that he should recognize in the development of human destinies the play of the contingent and the unforeseen.

GEORGE FORT MILTON
defines the historian as one who builds a causeway of tested truth across an ocean of myth and hypothesis.

HISTORY AS A MAJOR SPORT

PROBABLY it is because history is the most vital branch of human knowledge that the writing of it is so satisfying an intellectual adventure. At least it has been my own experience that the quest for the truth as to men, events and epochs, and recording one's conception of it in documented history, can prove a major sport surpassed in zest and sense of achievement by none I know.

Nor is this strange, for in its record of human experience history illumines man's struggle with nature, records his attempts at social co-operation and dramatizes his development against handicaps. The study is broad enough to portray the growth of ideas and cultures, and yet its exactitudes are such that research can be focussed on the splendors of a prince or the battle tragedy of an afternoon.

A reflective reading of the record of the past affords food for the mind, stimulus for the emotion, broadened horizons for the imagination and illumination for philosophy itself. But over and above this, there is delight in the quarrying of history's building stones, fascination in seeking causal relationships and satisfaction in breaking through the outer crust of fact to the truth behind it, to say nothing of the intellectual elation in discerning the why as well as the how of the event. Such cruises of discovery bring the working historian a sense of achievement and creation.

Such have been the sought for satisfactions which have inspired Gibbon, Macaulay, Froude, Acton, Beveridge, and other notabilities of the craft in the labors the results of which have so greatly adorned the firmament of the historian.

It may be of interest to follow the techniques by which documented history comes into being. Probably the starting-point of any special work is that the historical student comes to have a definite dissatisfaction with the content or the form of the depiction of some particular aspect or epoch of man's history. It might be the description of Cromwell's protectorate, or the cultural characteristics of the Greek city-state, or the history of European morals from the fall of Rome to the fall of the Bastille, or the origins of and responsibilities for the American Civil War: In regard to any of these, or a myriad others, the historian might conclude that the existing record is unsatisfactory, and that it is his duty to do the work anew.

His dissatisfaction might arise from a feeling that the accepted standard authority is infused with author prejudice, and shows an effort to make the worse seem the better reason. Or again, granting the propriety of the prior authors' subjective attitude, much important new material may have been uncovered since they wrote. Furthermore, the historian might be urged to his task by feeling that the picture as presented is distorted because essential and discoverable types of material have been left unfound and unapplied; or, finally, because he thinks that prior studies have failed in analysis and proportion. Usually several of these motives co-operate to persuade the historian to a specific labor.

It might be added that each new generation sees the past through fresh eyes, and so interprets yesterday in terms of today. Not only does this involve the translation of yesterday's prose into the current vocabulary, but the discovery in the great actors of yesterday of the identical compulsions and economic urges of the present day. This fact alone — the continuing need for our interpreting us to ourselves through clothing present ideas and emotions of today in the cerements of the past — assures a constant stream of new examinations and interpretations of history.

In a sense, each generation colors the past anew with the subjectivity of the immediate epoch. With sincere and conscientious practitioners of the art this constitutes no conscious distortion: such historians revere the classic unities of truth, and seek consciously to exclude completely any subjective prejudice or bias. But the historian's mental processes, like those of his fellows, are chiefly performed on the subconscious levels, only a small fraction occurring in the full illuminated areas of reasoned logic. Therefore, whatever may be the impartiality and objectivity with which historians seek to impress their work, they cannot escape the powerful subjective colorations of their backgrounds.

In the nature of things, a completely objective history would be a mere catalogue of all the facts of the particular relation, so encyclopediac that it could no more be written than read. Selection, therefore, is imperative, and selection involves judgment, calling for the rejection of this fact and the retention of that one; or, if both be retained, for according greater weight to one than to the other. This problem of choice calls for standards for weighing and selection, thus introducing the subjective element into the objective quest. The most the historian can do is deliberately to seek to safeguard his standards; to keep them, so far as he is conscious of them, free from prejudice and passion, and to have as his purpose not the proving of a hypothesis but the search for truth.

So much for the motives animating the historian in the backbreaking labors of writing documented history. Three main processes are involved in the task. To begin with, one must assemble the material upon which to base the text. Not only does this call for the examination of the pertinent periodical files, books and official reports and records. Even more importantly, the searcher needs an almost intuitive sense of the true shape of the record he is seeking, and a constructive imagination to enable him to uncover the new evidence essential to giving his new picture of the truth.

The second stage involves the historian's careful study, analysis, and judgment as to the reliability of particular data, or interpretations of their meaning. In connection with the 'corrupt bargain' charges, what weight shall one give Henry Clay's defense of his motives in electing John Quincy Adams President and then becoming his Secretary of State? Did John C. Calhoun's desire to reprimand Old Hickory for seizing Pensacola really lead to 1832's Democratic fissures, with its eventual issue of a Southern secession party, or was thus but the precipitating agent of changes growing out of the structural and functional characteristics of American society? Did Stephen A. Douglas really hazard the peace of America on a presidential bid, as Anti-Slavery politicians charged in the Appeal of the Independent Democrats, or was that incendiary document merely issued to fuse a new party in the crucible of hate? Was Lincoln's 'House Divided' the prophetic utterance of an American seer, or an adroit new issue on which to sustain a party whose *raison d'être* was gone? These questions, and a myriad like them, occupy the historian's mind as he fills the rôle of patient judge passing upon evidence.

In the third task, that of the actual literary composition, the historian is under severe compulsions. Like novelists, poets, philosophers and other writers, he is beset with the necessity to communicate; otherwise he would amass his information and spin his theories for his own private satisfaction. But this necessity of communication forces him to make the same psychological appeals as does the novelist. Both must have a key to open the door to attention, and interest is always the ideal key. Historical interest is not too difficult to arouse, for history itself is no dead thing but the re-creation of a real world; its men and women are of flesh and blood and their problems and passions are quite as real and vital as are those of our own generation; its societies are as fascinating in their similarities as in their differences from our own world.

The historian's task is to capture the ghosts of yesterday, and breathe into them the breath of life — a task requiring style as well as understanding, and calling for the marriage of scholarship and art. Yet it is a rôle made peculiarly difficult because the historian is denied the creative craftsman's liberty to follow the free range of his imagination. Confronted with a fixed mass of materials, the historian must cast them into moving and persuasive literary form. The tapestry of life he weaves must be in as brilliant colors and portray as moving scenes as those presented by the novelist — but the historian must use the old thread of fact. Should the reading interest flag, he cannot invent some new and striking scene to rejuvenate attention; the bond-servant of his material, he must build his mosaic out of the truth.

Let me illustrate these three phases of historical composition out of my own experience. It was during work upon a history of the consequences of the American Civil War that I first felt the need for reappraising the causes of that struggle. The part chance played in Reconstruction, the rôle of unpredictables and imponderables in the Impeachment outcome, raised serious doubts as to the analogous claim that the Civil War was inevitable. Soon after I began to burrow into the genetics of the War, it became plain that rival absolutes held sway in the period of the War's gestation and the Aristotelian mean between Abolition and Secession had been given but slight heed.

Soon two challenging questions presented themselves: To begin with, were the Absolutists right about the inevitability of the conflict? And again, if not, why had the present generation of historical scholars been able to do little more than hint the truth, without persuasive documentation? These intriguing questions led me into a historical job that took four years.

Now in the common run of things few mortals have so many mortgages upon their time as does the provincial newspaper publisher who must be at once editor, business man and factory executive, a job requiring just about twenty-four hours a day. Such a life has many satisfactions but leisure for scholarly research is not among them. At any event, all my historical work had to be performed from eight in the evening until midnight. The fatigues of the process, however, had their eventual reward.

Before I had been long at the task, it appeared that a main

reason for the apparent neglect of the middle-ground position was the inadequacy of data about it and its champions. It should be understood that different kinds of historical evidence have varying usefulness. The immediate, intimate record a participant in an event makes by diary entry or private letter is the most useful of all sources. Next in value is the account given in some contemporary newspaper, magazine, speech or debate; its worth, however, is often diminished because it is a formal and purposeful public presentation. Even less dependable is an individual's recollections years after the event, for usually these have grown dim from time or have suffered distortion because of subsequent events. Least useful of all is the mythology with which later generations often seek to justify inherited political prejudices.

While a few historians content themselves with the published document, the diplomatic note, or full-dress debate, such formal records seldom illuminate inner purpose. One who seeks the why of an event usually finds it necessary to discover the statesman off his guard, and for this one needs private diary or personal correspondence to supply the human background of the event.

Looking over the records of the 'Fifties I found more than enough intimate material about the great extremists. Many were the collections of private papers of the vanguard of Secession, for the embattled Southrons had preserved each vatic syllable and faded anecdote of Davis and Calhoun. Similarly the vast band of Lincolnian idolators had winnowed the Emancipator's memorabilia; Sumner's letters were preserved in due pomposity, along with those of Garrison, Phillips, Trumbull, Washburne, and Chase. Even 'Beast' Butler's multitudinous correspondence has been edited and put in libraries the nation over. But of the statesmen who had cried 'a plague on both your houses' the intimate record was slight indeed. The most important source available was the papers of John J. Crittenden, a stalwart Kentucky Conservative. But of the main group of Northern Democrats, the men who had almost won their effort to postpone the war, the yield was practically nil.

Thereupon I commenced a search; most of all it was desirable to discover the papers of Stephen A. Douglas, the great man of the epoch. A veritable human lodestone, Douglas attracted to himself a personal political party reaching every section of the nation, and became the focus of the effort to persuade peaceable adjustment. His papers, if extant, would almost certainly reveal the breadth and depth of the Conservative appeal.

Initial inquiries were disappointing; there had been a fire in Washington after the Little Giant's death, and the report was that all his private papers had been burned up. However, two Douglas grandsons lived in Greensboro, North Carolina. A visit there yielded the lively satisfaction of their friendship. One of them made available a rare parcel of letters Douglas had written home when, as a beardless boy, he went West to make his own way in the world. Soon the other, poking around in an old outhouse, came across an old packing-box. When it was hauled out one Saturday afternoon in March, 1931, and opened, my eyes feasted on hundreds of bundles of letters, each packet neatly tied in tape. I can remember to this day the tremendous thrill of that discovery — it was a major part of the Little Giant's papers! These were the key to the magic door of the 'Fifties, and that key was in my hands.

Discovery was the first step, making use of it the next one. There were fully twenty-five thousand letters in the box; each one must be deciphered and read, its matter of consequence discerned and put into adequate note. Then, too, time was important. It did not take long to secure an office, rent two typewriters, and hire a stenographic staff. Then for six eye-dimming weeks it was my task to decipher letters, mark passages to be copied, and do all other things needful in extracting the heart and essence of a great correspondence.

Of course the papers of statesmen of that day, before typewriters or duplicating devices, consisted practically altogether of letters received. Indeed, this was a great merit, for one read that stream of incoming reports, appeals, and suggestions with the uncanny feeling of having one's finger on the pulse of an epoch and a cause.

Finally the task was done and I came home, my notebooks bulging with a new record of the 'Fifties — one so explosive in the character of its evidence that I had no hesitation in terming the struggle which followed Sumter as a 'needless war.' For the Douglas papers filled the great gap theretofore existing in the evidence; they threw new light on the motives and techniques by which the Ultra minorities in both sections manipulated official machinery, and showed that the masses of the people, South and North alike, did not want this politicians' war.

But it was not enough to have found these letters. The very fact of their discovery called for checking of evidence, testing of statements, examination of opposing viewpoints, to say nothing of the actual writing itself. It was important to find Douglas's responses to his chief correspondents. To do this, I classified the letters by the States of the writers' residence, sending these lists to the appropriate State Historical Societies, prominent newspapers, etc., asking their aid in finding living descendants of those who had worked with the Little Giant. Over a thousand such letters went out, and this I backed by personal tours of investigation. Some of the resultant discoveries were most valuable. For example, in Springfield, Illinois, I found Douglas's correspondence with General John A. McClernand, at first his rival and then one of his staunchest Congressional aides. There, too, grandsons of William H. Lanphier, the Little Giant's ablest editor, made the whole rich Lanphier correspondence available. In the middle 'Fifties Douglas had established the Chicago *Times*, putting James W. Sheahan at the editorial helm, and in 1860 Sheahan prepared the Little Giant's campaign biography. In Chicago I had the good fortune to find Sheahan's son; he turned over to me another treasure-trove of Douglas's letters.

Quests of this type call for the detective about as much as the historian. Careful running down of random leads is essential and often rewarded, but sometimes success is just sheer luck. There was the case of the Sanders letters. George N. Sanders was an eërie Kentucky editor-politician who wanted Douglas to lead a political revolution to throw the Old Fogies out. But Sanders acted like a bull in the china shop, a cause which allied all other candidates against Douglas, whose denials and disavowals were received with scorn. I became convinced that, but for Sanders, the Little Giant would have been elected President in 1852. The common view was that the Senator was directing every move of the mischief, but I did not believe it — such a course was altogether out of character with Douglas's own technique, and I felt sure that the latter must have made frantic efforts to halt his friend's mad course. Of this there was inferential evidence in Sanders's letters to Douglas. But to prove the point I must have the Little Giant's answers.

Soon I found that a batch of Douglas's letters to Sanders had been sold in New York in 1915. The auction gallery exhumed its ledger record of purchasers, by means of which I traced and secured copies of half of the original collection. But apparently the rest had vanished in thin air. It happened that that indexer extraordinary, Mr. Joseph Greenbaum, of New York, recalled that, years before, a bookbinder friend had found a scrapbook of Lincoln items. On the chance it might have some useful data, Mr. Greenbaum set to work to trace it. After months of search, it came to light that the scrapbook had been presented to the public library at Watertown, Connecticut, and that not only was it a scrapbook of old clippings, but that also it contained eight letters from Douglas to George Sanders. These enabled me to reconstruct the whole story of the tragedy of that campaign. Had it not been for this Kentucky marplot, Douglas might well have been President in 1852, perhaps the Missouri Compromise would not have been repealed and there would have been no Civil War!

After collection of material comes the task of judgment, about as difficult as discovery of fact. Here the historian must be an expert on the reliability of handwriting, have some knowledge of the credibility of witnesses and be a shrewd searcher into the motives of man. It is also necessary for him to become thoroughly imbued with the problems and personalities of the age of which he writes so that, in a sense, he is actually reliving the days gone by. Through thus recapturing the sense of historical participation, he re-creates the reality of the problems of the past generation and makes them once more living things.

It would be wrong to give the impression that each of the three processes of material gathering, analysis, and composition is separate in point of time. At least, so far as the present writer is concerned, the three went on simultaneously, and with each particular episode there was an intense effort to do all three at once.

The actual writing might be described as the building of an island of ascertainment, next constructing a second island, and then building a bridge between the two. When my attention was concentrated on the Compromise of 1850, I assembled all material thereon, tested and fitted it, put it into prose, and drafted and redrafted the account. Probably there were a dozen rewritings of the story; but once finished, and given due polish as to style, I proceeded on to Douglas's bid for the Presidency in 1852.

In this fashion one proceeds steadily across the wide ocean of myth and hypothesis, carefully building a causeway of tested truth. There is no better way to work out an appropriate framework for a period than by building forward step by step, mastering each episode as one proceeds. And as one goes forward, one's subconscious mind classifies all the variant facts, and when the whole work is done one has an almost intuitive sense of appropriate proportions, by which to guide final recasting.

Once all the islands are built and bridges put in, the need for integration leads to months of revision and rearrangement. Then it is that the spirit groans most mournfully. After one has read and edited a single chapter a dozen times or so, it requires considerable courage to sit down to it with a battery of sharpened pencils, to try to cut from it a space saving of a hundred words a page. And yet, when publishers din in your ears the words of Michelangelo, 'The More the Marble Wastes, the More the Statue Grows,' one comes almost to believe it. Even so, there is a real pang when one forces one's own pencil to strike out a paragraph which represents the fruits of two months' careful investigation; or when a purple passage is doomed to slaughter as surplusage.

Let us say no more of these spiritual travails of the final stages of historical composition. Likewise let us draw the veil of silence over the agonies of proof-reading, and then of finding in the printed volume typographical errors which stick out like a sore thumb. Eventually the work is done and Leviathan is born. It must be admitted that when one finishes such a work, one asks: 'Why did I ever undertake such toil?' But this feeling is not long-lived. Soon it is overcome by the feeling of mastery, the feeling that one has really plumbed to the depths of an epoch. The historian persuades himself that, through finding how and why men acted as they did a century ago, one suspects a little better what are the mainsprings of our contemporary society. At any rate, permit me to nominate the writing of history as a major sport for all who are interested in what makes the wheels go round in the whirligig of Life.

ROUSSEAU

I write in my brain as I walk among rocks or in woods. I need torrents, pines, dark forests, mountains, rough paths to climb by precipices that fill me with fear.

WILLIAM BUTLER YEATS

I must speak of things that come out of the common consciousness, where every thought is like a bell with many echoes.

MARCEL PROUST

Our passions shape our books, repose writes them in the intervals.

BALZAC

It is true that I go out little and sit at my work for twenty hours.

MONTAIGNE

I speak on paper as I do to the first person I meet.

A. E. HOUSMAN

Experience has taught me, when I am shaving, to keep watch over my thoughts, because if a line of poetry strays into my memory, my skin bristles so that the razor ceases to act.

EDWARD J. O'BRIEN
examines 'that Cinderella of American literature' and sees hope in our creative discontent.

THE AMERICAN SHORT STORY

IT WAS not only with pleasure, but with a sense of having rediscovered my country, that I returned to New York in 1934 after an absence of ten years. So much water had passed under the bridges during that time that I felt that I had come to a new world of writers, a new generation of writers to whose advent I had looked forward, but the significance of whose achievement certainly neither I nor anyone else could have foreseen ten years ago. There has been a quickening of comprehension in American life that is marvelous, and that quickening of comprehension is evident in the American short story writer.

I am not a literary critic. There is no time to spare in this country at this moment for criticism, although there are many pretenders to the critical armchair. I am a private in the ancient and honorable army, the very ancient and very honorable army, of crossing sweeps. The profession is so ancient that it has been almost forgotten. It has been displaced by traffic lights in New York, and the crossing sweep is gone with his broom with which he cleared away the mud. He has joined the ranks of those whom the machine has destroyed or destined to unemployment. That is sad, perhaps, but there are a few of us left, and I am proud to say that there is work for us to do.

Everybody in this country, whether or not otherwise gainfully employed, has at some time or other conceived the idea that it would be a fine thing to write short stories. That it would be a fine thing to write short stories of integrity is believed by quite a few, and in the eyes of God the others do not matter. But in the eyes of the American people of twenty-one years ago, when I was beginning to look at the American short story, and undertook to edit the first volume of 'The Best Short Stories,' the reverse was true. In 1914 when I was an innocent boy and wanted to examine the American short story, those few who wanted to write stories of integrity were despised. That seemed strange to me and I am still wondering why it was so, and why it is still so to a considerable degree. But in the main I have found out, for my broom has told me. In that year, 1914, I bought a new broom and began to sweep crossings.

Twenty-one years ago, when I first began to read the American short story published in all kinds of magazines, from the pretentious commercial magazines, through the pulp and political ones, the smaller ones, and on down, the situation that confronted the innocent reader was as follows:

The short story resided on four main avenues. 'First Avenue' was the avenue of plots. Plot was a curious institution designed to be erected as a framework of steel, unbreakable, on which you hung things; you began with 'plot.' On 'First Avenue' there were rows and rows of plots.

On 'Second Avenue' there were rows and rows of types — not people, just types. There were the types of commercial integrity or nobility as conceived by the successful business man, or something quaint, such as an actor would present in portraying 'character' in a melodrama.

'Third Avenue' was the avenue of local colour. This was rather an expensive avenue for the short story writer. If he had distinguished himself on the first two avenues, he could go to a magazine or editor and get the necessary wherewithal for the opportunity to travel through the world and look at 'local colour' for a year or so. It never occurred to him to look at his own soil, his home environment, or his own soul, for his local colour.

'Fourth Avenue' there was no getting away from! It was the 'surprise ending.' Every ingenuity was used to shock and surprise you, but the trouble was that you could never be shocked twice by the same ending or the same story, which made this avenue somewhat ephemeral.

The story built on these four avenues is still written in this country, but it is a short story which is dead, absolutely dead. It has been killed. It is still being written, but it doesn't know that it is dead.

The new type of writer is quite different. He is alert, avid of expression — not for its own sake, but as something which clarifies his own mind and enriches his own life. The man or woman who is interesting and important among the new writers is not pretentious, but simply one who writes simply, who registers what he sees, transferring it into terms which are such that they appeal to other people. He writes with creative discontent, has emerged from the old false romanticism, and looks at things with a cool, direct view.

He is bombarded all the time, to be sure, by all sorts of unrelated sense impressions, those shocks which we encounter every moment in this modern inferno, but he finds that there is a security within himself that is a good guide if he accepts life as it is and translates it into disinterested art.

He is in some danger of a new kind of standardization, if he takes the easiest road, but I have a feeling that the last two or three years of the depression have simplified life for us a great deal, and made the direct human material much more accessible.

In England the public is quite as much interested in the young American short story as in the young English short story. In a magazine called 'New Stories,' which I am editing in conjunction with five English authors, we have had to agree to set up a higher standard for judging the American short story than for judging the English short story, or we should have no space left to print any English stories. Doesn't that suggest that whatever there is here in America may have a creative influence on the older European life, and may even help us to pay back some of the debt which we owe to the older tradition of our language?

Since 1819, the year in which Washington Irving published 'The Sketch Book,' the short story has been the literary form which has mirrored most closely the course of American life and the development of American character. At its best, it has always been the least self-conscious form in which the American writer has chosen to express himself, and therefore the most revealing to the foreign observer. If we read a large and historically illustrative collection of these stories, it is fascinating to trace the change in folkways from the severe pioneer life of the early days of the republic to the highly developed industrial life of the present day.

Before 1892, American life was practically homogeneous.

The population was predominantly Anglo-Saxon, definitely provincial, and pioneering in its general outlook. Life still had an open and unconquered material frontier, and the energies of the American people were almost exclusively directed toward the consolidation and development of what it had already acquired and the final conquest of the continent which it had explored and opened out with such rapidity and energy. American short stories written before 1892 are almost without exception preoccupied with the life of a pioneer civilization. They are for the most part all of one piece and woven out of rough serviceable material. Such exceptions as there are to this rule are the work of artists who are either in revolt against pioneer folkways and therefore inclined to portray the life of their land in a mood of rejection, or of artists whose nostalgia for the more ordered and traditional ways of Europe has weakened their art to the point where it is content to be a pale mirror of a Europe which they have visited but whose rooted life has rejected them. The artist in revolt, a Poe or a Melville, is sometimes more significant than the artist who has accepted American life. The writer homesick for Europe, however, is usually frustrate and provincial. His work, when we read it now, is seen to date. It is faded like the woolwork of our great-grandmothers. Who, for example, now reads N. P. Willis — the American Byron, as they used to call him?

It would be a grievous error to suppose that the short story of the pioneer period had no roots and no traditions. On the contrary, it was profoundly conditioned by the Anglo-Saxon racial memory. Before 1892, this racial memory was vital and instinctive, so vital and instinctive that it was fierce and proud. Since 1892, the rapid influx of immigrants from all European countries has tended to efface the Anglo-Saxon tradition very rapidly, and it is now waning almost to extinction. Its last strongholds are to be found in New England and the South. Linked to this racial memory as one of the two springs of its vitality, the earlier American short story owed much to the conflict of man with nature while wresting from destiny a new and untamed land. That, of course, is the epic theme of pioneer life. As Washington Irving and Nathaniel Hawthorne illustrate the power of racial memory as a shaping literary force, so Bret Harte and Hamlin Garland illustrate the conflict of man with nature on the frontier.

Pioneer life is unpropitious to outstanding literary merit. Poe and Herman Melville, for example, are classical examples of what happens to a writer of great individual genius in a frontier civilization. Pioneers have no sympathy to waste on artists. They follow the law of the tribe. In such a society, the artist is expected to be one of the tribe in everything, or he will find himself cut off from the tribe by reason of its instinct for protective solidarity against the perils of the new and strange. The pioneer's partial regression to the primitive is a necessary condition of his survival, and primitive life, as any anthropologist will tell you, is a network of imperatives conceived as taboos.

The Civil War profoundly altered this pioneer tradition east of the Mississippi. It exhausted too much of the nation's vitality, and the youth of American literature, in which Irving and Hawthorne, Poe and Melville, and such minor, but outstanding, short story writers as William Austin and FitzJames O'Brien, had written great short stories and had set the pattern of this literary form for other countries, drew on towards a sober and apparently undistinguished middle age. West of the Mississippi the life of the pioneer was still an actuality for another generation. Life was still moving westward and men were still faced with the problem of subduing nature to their own needs.

The year 1892 seems to mark the time when the last frontier was to all intents and purposes closed, and the World's Fair held in Chicago not only commemorated America's consciousness of the fact, but served to emphasize the end of a purely Anglo-Saxon United States. There had been much Irish and German immigration in the previous half-century, but not enough to disturb seriously the homogeneity of the American people. The Irish sat below the salt; the Germans kept more or less clannishly to themselves. Other European races were in a negligible minority.

Between 1892 and 1914, however, the whole character and texture of American life was profoundly altered by the rapid growth of industrial construction and the consequent demand for cheap labour which encouraged the immigration of great numbers of Southern and Eastern Europeans. The literary and cultural supremacy of the Anglo-Saxon was now definitely challenged, as millions of newcomers arrived who brought with them a wide variety of different racial traditions. The problem of assimilating so many different traditions seemed insoluble. At first, the dominant Anglo-Saxon community sought to subdue and crush these new alien cultures, to enforce conformity, and to level down all imaginative life to the sterile inbred provincial dullness to which it had reduced itself. This process was called Americanization.

The twenty-two years between 1892 and 1914 were years of standardization, not only in industry, but also in education and in the arts as well. It was the generation which invented mass-production and which was proud of its invention. It mass-produced machinery, it mass-produced minds, and, of course, it mass-produced short stories. The American short story of the generation before the war was constructed by blue print to engineering formula, assembled from spare parts, and certified as classical by American universities. It made money and it satisfied an ever-increasing demand. A friend of mine once described it succinctly as 'a fairy-tale for grown-ups.' Its demands suffocated more than one genius. Stephen Crane fought a losing battle against the stream all his life; Ambrose Bierce and Jack London succumbed without fighting. The greatest short story writer of the period, Henry James, was an avowed expatriate. Here talent was stifled, and mediocrity reigned supreme amid the plaudits of the multitude. In 1914, the American short story had gained the whole world, and, it seemed to every dispassionate observer, had lost its own soul. It was like the versatile Mrs. Amyot in Edith Wharton's short story, 'The Pelican,' of whom it was said: 'It was her art of transposing second-hand ideas into first-hand emotions that so endeared her to her feminine listeners.'

There was a paradox in all this. The vitality and apparently inexhaustible energy of American life was to be felt in all these stories. They sprang up like bracken on newly cleared timberland. The restless curiosity of America is apparent in them as well as that democratic interest in every man and his neighbor out of which a valuable literature of interpretation might grow. The most restless, the most curious and the most human of these writers was O. Henry, whose best stories are extremely readable by reason of their humour, versatility, appeal to curiosity, and element of surprise. O. Henry may be said to have invented the 'surprise ending' which made each of his stories a new cocktail for the public to taste. O. Henry's zest for life, his bravado, his easy comradeship, his drollery, his capacity to seize the elements of romance in a standardized civilization, will probably suffice to preserve twenty-five or thirty of his stories from oblivion. They are certainly consummate journalism, and O. Henry's journalism not infrequently becomes literature. It was his unique distinction to see New York as Bagdad-on-the-Subway.

An O. Henry or a Jack London was the best that the American short story had to offer us during the first fifteen or sixteen years of the twentieth century. There were many more pretentious writers, but they were all derivative. Henry James had many disciples who mastered his technique, but who lacked his sensitivity, and there were many regionalist writers who were honest craftsmen. Few of them, however, seemed able to apprehend life directly and to write vividly with their eyes on the object. Most honest efforts failed through their preoccupation with one or more of the four prevailing American heresies, which I have mentioned above and which may be characterized briefly as the heresy of 'types,' the heresy of 'local colour,' the heresy of 'plot,' and the heresy of the 'surprise ending.'

The heresy of 'types' was a curious feature of most American stories. The standardization of life achieved its own monotony, and in the United States interest in character is likely to be limited either to the familiar recognition of what is usual or the observation of what is held to be quaint. There was consequently no wish to observe life freshly and simply. Characterization was deliberately limited to broad strokes of identification, or else to a condescending description of the 'quaintness' of what were regarded as the lower races. The heresy of 'local colour' was due to the writer's self-conscious search for a background. Popular short story writers went to Morocco, to the Caucasus, to the South Sea Islands, with letters of credit supplied by complaisant editors, with the object of finding that adequate background for life which they seemed unable to find at home. The usual result was that the background dwarfed the foreground, and the characters became two-dimensional figures like paper dolls.

The heresy of 'plot' was more serious. It became an accepted canon among editors that a good short story should have an elaborate and intricately constructed plot full of action with unforeseen happenings. The result was to devitalize characterization and to substitute for flesh and blood galvanically animated puppets whose shadow-play was supposed to interest the spectator keenly. American universities added schools of short story writing to their curricula, and in these schools elaborately codified rules were laid down for 'motivating plot development.' The results, of course, were solemnly absurd. 'Plot' conceived on these lines made the obligatory 'surprise ending' borrowed from O. Henry ridiculous. The 'surprise ending' became an inevitable formula in which the 'surprise' was always foreseen.

During the War, conscription brought many young American writers to Europe for a year or two. Influential critics, notably Randolph Bourne and Van Wyck Brooks, had been teaching the younger men that America lacked a 'usable past.' After the War, many of these men remained in Paris and Paris became the Mecca of most of the others. This had two effects, one good and one bad. On the one hand, it served to make potential artists creatively restless and disposed to inquire into themselves. On the other hand, it tended to make them undervalue their home background and folkways. Fortunately, two important short story writers emerged who were not only able to absorb the free and disinterested ways of the European artist, but who were also intensely preoccupied with the texture of American life.

Sherwood Anderson and Ernest Hemingway have set an example which is already leading the American short story back into the ways it had forsaken. They are both major writers to be set unhesitatingly beside the great masters of the art. Anderson's 'The Triumph of the Egg' yields nothing to Chekhov; Hemingway's 'Fifty Grand' stands firm beside Mérimée's 'Mateo Falcone.' Each has written a dozen stories of equal calibre. What is their essential achievement, and why does it seem as if they have been the liberating influence of a new and richer American literature? Well, to begin with, they are the most essential Americans since Lincoln and Walt Whitman. They entirely lack the self-consciousness which vitiates so much serious American writing. They are content to use the simplest materials and instinctively distrust that 'literary' writing which is the mark of all provincial literatures. They are alike in their definite revolt against the highly mechanized short story of commerce, and they have communicated this spirit of revolt to a great many young writers who have fine achievement already to their credit. Best of all, their stories are already a strong fertilizing influence in many European countries, and I cannot help believing that they will have a freshening effect ultimately on English short story writers who stand precisely in need of this fresh simple apprehension of reality which is transforming American letters.

During the past five years a new generation of American short story writers has appeared, the body of whose work is in my opinion unchallengably the best now being written in the world. Most of them have been influenced by Sherwood Anderson and Ernest Hemingway. None of them are disciples.

They have found it extremely difficult to get their work published by the older established magazines, and therefore they have founded their own magazines which, despite the depression, seem to flourish.

This is the most interesting moment in the history of American letters, and the most interesting thing about it is that America is finding its soul through the interpretation of its life to its own people by the short story writers rather than by the poets. And it is the poetry of American life which its best short story writers are revealing with such simple honesty and dignity.

I should like to conclude these remarks by drawing the attention of the reader to the fact that there is no better way of learning to understand the life of the American people than by reading its better short stories. Sometimes it seems to me that I began to read American short stories almost exactly at the time that the modern American short story was born, and now that my series of books, 'The Best Short Stories,' has just passed its twenty-first birthday, I feel as if the short story also had come of age.

It is fascinating to look back over these twenty-one years and watch the steady and rapid development, not only of the short story itself, but of the consciousness of the American people of their own destiny as it has developed during this period. A generation ago the serious short story was the Cinderella of American literature, despised and rejected by her more fortunate brothers and sisters. Now she is in full possession of her birthright, and the American public realizes at last that a volume of short stories can be quite as entertaining as, and far more varied than, a novel.

One hundred and fifty volumes of short stories worthy of an intelligent reader are published in this country now every year.

It has been proven to me, if it is not yet clear to the average bookseller and publisher, that a good volume of short stories is profitable in its own right, and I think the reader will agree with me on reflection that there is a wide field of unexplored country before him in current volumes of short stories which is well worthy of his attention.

JOHN KEATS

If poetry comes not as naturally as the leaves to a tree, it had better not come at all.

CARL SANDBURG

Poetry is the achievement of the synthesis of hyacinths and biscuits.

MAX EASTMAN

It appears that a poet in history is divine, but a poet in the next room is a joke.

LONGFELLOW

Perhaps the greatest lesson which the lives of literary men teach us is told in a single word: Wait!

LOUISA M ALCOTT

Work for twenty years and then you may find some day that you have a style and a place of your own.

OVID

Much have I written, but what I thought defective I have myself given to the flames, for their revision.

FRANCES FROST *looks upon poetry as a sort of cosmic shorthand, able to express in a few words the core, the substance of life.*

THE ETERNAL APPRENTICE

IN A sense, it is one of the most difficult things in the world for a poet to speak of poetry, although he is apt to swamp any willing listener or opponent in argument with theories, ideas, technical problems, or anything else pertaining to the subject in which he is most interested and about which he can never become wholly objective.

I can argue with a fellow poet forever; I can quarrel over the respective values of the lyric and the epic; I can swear that the lyric can be made into an epic, by which statement I draw down upon my head the wrath of all the heavens, including the Olympian; I can untangle in my own mind snagged technical points simply by getting into a good fight with somebody else about those problems.

But when I am asked to write or speak formally of poetry, I am tongue-tied with fright, with doubt, with humility. What can I say of it? What can anyone say of it that is not inherent in the poetry itself? It is a fever in the blood of him who must write it, it is a fine frenzy in his mind, it is the acute perception of his entire being transmuted — or translated — into the essence of speech — and it cannot be satisfactorily defined, if it can be defined at all. I like Housman's answer to someone who asked him for a definition of poetry: 'I can no more define poetry than a terrier can define a rat.' It is impossible to reduce authentic poetry to an imaginative or a scientific formula, in spite of the fact that poetry can be conceived out of H_2O or geometry or the light-years it takes for the bright white fire of Altair to reach this earth, or out of the chemical reaction of a field left fallow for a season. Being shorter than prose and more incisive, poetry is able to grasp briefly and sharply the undertones and overtones of human existence in its various forms. It is a sort of cosmic shorthand, able to express in a few words the core, the substance of life, as it is perceived and interpreted by the poet. Poetry finds the warm breath of a man made visible in freezing air; in the thud of his heart by night it knows his love or his loss; in his footprints over a wandering earth it reads his hunger for uncharted places; it spells out his soul's dark questioning, his body's brief delight. It knows his fear, his peace, his desire for knowledge; it probes his hope, his faith; it knows his glory and his defeat. Why ask what poetry is, when poetry is the answer?

The readers and lovers of poetry, and sometimes the critics of it, feel that the completed poem, the perfect poem, must have sprung full-fledged from the poet's mind. In rare instances this may prove to be the case, but more often only a fragment, a line, a stanza, appear in the poet's mind without any effort on his part, and he must go on and build his poem with extreme technical care, however urgent his thought and emotion may be. And whether his poem comes to him easily or whether he labors over it, it is imperative that he have his technique at his finger-tips; he must have studied poetry for years, he must have worked patiently, practicing, discarding, until he developed both skill and style. A poet may be born with talent or genius, and he may have some amount of instinctive technical ability, but he is not born with technical knowledge and that he must get for himself. And to that knowledge there is no end. The poet must be the eternal apprentice.

He must be his own most severe critic. Poetry is not only an art — it is a job and a tremendously exacting one. It demands that the poet be prepared to search for hours, days, weeks, for the right word, the exact word, the acute phrase, to control both his mind and his medium, to throw away what is not his best work, to write at high tension, making sure that the form of his poem is indigenous, growing out of the mingled thought and emotion, to polish every line with extreme care.

I become impatient with those kind people who say, 'Oh, how wonderful it must be to write poetry! — it just comes to you, doesn't it?' Of course it is wonderful and I am grateful, indeed, to whatever gods gave me a push in the direction of poetry; but it doesn't 'just come' painlessly, without travail, any more than a field can yield a harvest without first being ploughed, harrowed, sown and cultivated. Out of the field of my subconscious, where I have been planting the seeds of human experience since I drew my first breath and howled and was parked under the kitchen stove while the doctor worked over my mother — out of that field strange things have sprouted, sights, sounds, smells, contacts, ideas, loves, hates, hungers, to be translated into language, with that concentration of mind and heart which is half joy and half anguish. No, poems do not arrive out of nothing as it were, and if they did I believe the poet would be as astonished as would a woman if she were suddenly handed a baby and told she had produced it unbeknownst to herself.

It is true that there is some mystery about the urge and ability to write, whether the writing be prose or poetry; but there is as much mystery in painting or the composing of music. Why I *have* to write poetry, I don't know. Why the need, the relentless feverish urge to write is an active physical and spiritual distress, I don't know. Why, in actual composition, my mind selects one word and rejects another, I haven't the remotest idea, except that I think it may be partly instinct — whatever poetic instinct is! — and partly training. I disagree with Wordsworth's theory that poetry is emotion remembered in tranquillity; it presupposes that in tranquillity you have finished with that emotion... then how could you write about it with any sincerity or vigor? I don't know how it is with other poets, but for my part, if I remember an emotion, I remember it *with* emotion; I feel as strongly as I did at the moment of experience. If I recall coming out of the woods in a late afternoon and seeing the slanting sunlight luminous on the grassy stubble of a sloping field, I see that field, I feel as I felt then, excited, breathless, profoundly moved, and I write of it in a mood far from tranquil. But why I am able to write of it at all, I cannot say: I only know that I must.

This essay gives me the opportunity for disagreeing verbally with those who cry for *pure* poetry, by which term, as I understand it, they mean verse apparently devoid of meaning, but so rich in sensual imagery and color as to have upon the reader approximately the same effect as does music upon the ordinary listener. Whether or not the writers of pure poetry had some subtle and intricate meaning in mind, undiscovered even by poets, these gentlemen do not say. George Moore, for one, in his 'Anthology of Pure Poetry,' says that the less meaning a poem has, the purer it is. And Housman maintains, 'Meaning is of the intellect, poetry is not.... Blake's meaning is often unimportant or virtually non-existent, so that we can listen with all our hearing to his celestial tune....' I beg to disagree with both gentlemen. If poetry has neither emotional nor intellectual meaning, then it becomes nothing but verbal gymnastics, appealing only physically to the ear and to the eye. But even the purest poetry must draw upon the intellectual and emotional comprehension of the reader — the writer of it must know well the physical reaction of certain words and be aware of what both the reaction and the words call up in the mind or heart of the listener, and so be able to play upon his audience in such a fashion as to produce not only sensual pleasure but psychic satisfaction.

I believe that the best poetry, great poetry, is compounded of intellectual, emotional, and physical elements, imaginatively blended and written down with as much skill as is humanly possible. There is something to be said for the madness of poets — without it, they would scarcely be poets. It is the fine frenzy which I mentioned before; their perception of the visible world is acute, their sensitivity to their fellow beings is so heightened as to become anguish, their mortal and fatal struggle to understand and to translate into concrete speech the unknown, half-guessed-at significances of life becomes so violent that their clear and beautiful sanity seems madness to those who observe them from the safer borders of ordinary existence... and the only sanity in this world is a disciplined insanity.

AMY LOWELL

For books are more than books, they are the life
The very heart and core of ages past
The reason why men lived, and worked, and died,
The essence and quintessence of their lives.

ARCHIBALD MacLEISH
expresses the belief that the test of a poem is its power to withstand emotion.

EMOTION AND FORM IN POETRY

WHEN you say that poetry is an art you are supposed to speak pedantically and in a metaphoric sense. When you insist you are thought to be mad. For all the world — or rather all heirs of the English tradition — know that poetry is not an art at all. On the contrary it is a sort of oratorical utterance more or less allegorical which falls into the rhythmic speech of ecstasy, of exaltation, because its import is too awful for ordinary language. And poets are not artists but prophets or seers whose Messages are the only circumstances of importance about them. So Shakespeare is great for his knowledge of the human heart, and 'the quality that has preserved the tragic glory of the "Iliad,"' according to John Jay Chapman, 'is the huge enveloping piety behind it.' Or if one prefers a slightly more sophisticated statement, it is explained that poetry is a means of communicating or exciting emotion, and that the best poem is the poem that stirs up the most emotion in the reader. Both statements are wrong and both are fatuous, for both are instances of the apologizing and extenuating zeal which wrote the 'De Continentia Virgiliana' and which can no more endure today than it could in the Middle Ages the conception of art as an end, as a goal, in itself. But while the first justification of poetry, the prophetic justification, being put forth with all the cold-blooded ardor of Puritanism, is the more obstinate, the second, the emotional justification, offers a more convenient yardstick to the professional reviewer and is thus more often met with. Few poets whose work is clean and sure have escaped the impeachment of some sedulously sensitive reviewer who, not having been made to feel the emotion which he has previously associated with the subject, has at once concluded that the poem fails.

Emotion has its place in poetry as it has in painting. But its place is not that which the sensationalists give it. So far is it from being true that the test of a poem is its power to excite emotion that the exact contrary is the case. The test of a poem is its power to withstand emotion. The bad poem is the poem which has not crystallized, which remains raw emotion exciting emotion in the reader by its own excitement. The good poem is the poem which, whatever its origin, its raw material, has undergone the inexplicable metamorphosis; has *become*, has taken sensuous form, has turned into something as tangible as the Venus de Milo herself at the end of her long corridor in the Louvre. Perhaps the *material* of poetry is emotion: perhaps it is personal and not aesthetic emotion. But if that is so, the part played by emotion is the part played by the black cat in the fairy tale which, killed, turned into the fairy prince. To make anything out of the beast you must first get rid of it. The poem which results, if it is a poem, will not declare the emotions out of which it was made. Nor will it *stand for* them. Instead it will be a new thing which was perhaps originally an attempt to express emotion but which is now a poem. And that poem is all that concerns the reader.

The difficulty is obviously to make people understand that a poem is, in no mystical manner of speaking, a sensuous object, as real, as sensible as the bronze inkwell there on the desk. So many authoritative names are connected with the misuse of poetry for mere communication, mere expression, so many elderly Wordsworths exhibit their moral excellence in the anthologies, that it is all but impossible to come at the question at all. And the question is obviously one of form. So long as people talk about form in poetry as though it were a matter solely of metre, or metre and rhythm, or metre and rhythm and rhyme — as though, for instance, a sonnet were a 'form' — just so long form and content in poetry will be different and separate things, and poems will be discussed as though they were means of communicating elevated thoughts, and earnest young men will get perennially excited over the possibility of writing a first-rate poem in couplets — a question of no importance to anyone but the technicians and, at this date, of little enough importance to them.

But it is easier to say what form in poetry is not than to say with any hope of inclusive accuracy what it is. Poetry is an art existing in time but not in time only. Its structure is the line of a succession — something like the musician's melodic line — but the units of the succession are three-dimensional. Its form, in other words, is no such metaphysical anatomy as the pattern of a thought. Anything but that. There is a substantiation of thought in sense. The very words of poetry are so used that the words as sounds, as shapes, absorb and contain their meanings as symbols, tend to *become* their meanings, to such an extent that untranslatableness into other words, even of the same language, is one of the classic tests of poetic style. And the form of the poem as a whole results from the relation to each other in time — rhythm here being what proportion is in the visual arts — of words or groups of words which have undergone such a metamorphosis; of thought which has precipitated, crystallized; of images perceptible to the sense — by which is meant, perceptible to the whole body as an instrument of sense and not to the eyes alone. But those who can feel the sensuous reality, the finality, the all but tangible existence of a great poem, have no need of definition. And the rest of the world will go on in spite of reproof or remonstrance peering and peeping through the words of poetry at the emotional experience of the poet, or his understanding of the emotional experiences of others, or his Message, as though they had before them the verbal knotholes of prose; they will go on denying that poetry is an art — or rather that a poem is a work of art, for in art there are no rules but only instances; and they will end with the moral edification or the titillation of the emotions which is the vulgarian's complete reward. For those who try to see through a poem usually succeed. But the poem remains as blank to them as glass.

1925

STANLEY UNWIN

There is nothing very mysterious about a publisher's office.

JOHN FARRAR

To try to define a good book is impossible.

CURTIS BROWN

Whether a book floats or not depends upon the book itself.

HARRY HANSEN

Publishers get closer to authors than critics or even fellow authors.

ERSKINE CALDWELL

All I am I attribute to my dislike of reading books.

EDWARD WEEKS

There is something to be said for remaining within a room of one's own and allowing one's books to do the talking.

HERBERT AGAR traces the fine dividing line which exists between the literature of moral exhortation and the literature of economics.

JUST WHY ECONOMICS

I

THE bookstores are full of works on economics today. For the most part the professional economists turn up their noses, saying that this is trash. And for the most part the general public refuses the books which the economists think worthy; for such books (when they are comprehensible) seem inhumanly abstract, seem to be written about a world which might please a mathematician, but which has slight resemblance to the disorderly home of man.

And yet — economics is neither a vain nor an unimportant subject. It is hardly an exaggeration to say that, unless the plain man can acquire some economic insight, our whole grandiose system may soon be brought to the ground. It has become so desperately complicated that merely to analyze its workings is a task for a highly trained mind. One result of this complication is that the system has begun to look easy to a number of minds which are not noted for their training. To see the system whole has become a profession; but any man can see a little part of it and call that part the whole. Many men are doing this today, and are telling us with glad cries that we could just as well all be rich. The plain man, who can find no books on economics that are both 'sound' and readable, can hardly be blamed if he begins to believe these happy amateurs. He can hardly be blamed; but he will most certainly be punished. For if he believes them, he will refuse consent to any government that seeks to act on the true facts. He will insist on a new set of 'facts' — facts in keeping with the 'economy of abundance' which is reputed to be just round the corner. And finance-capitalism is so precarious a machine that we dare not handle it ignorantly. Handled with our utmost skill it is clumsy and onerous enough. Handled by a group of cheerful cranks, it may bog down suddenly. The result would not be 'abundance.'

It is important, then, that there should be a literature of economics that the plain man can understand, and which his political representatives can understand. One does not need to be a friend of finance-capitalism to see that the worst way of curing it is to wreck it outright. After such a cure even the most righteous of us might starve to death. But in order to cure it in a more agreeable way, one must first understand it; so a true literature of economics is a genuine need. To what extent does such a literature exist? And to what extent could it be called into being if an intelligent demand were created? The first step toward answering these questions is to distinguish between economics, politics, morals, and economic history. The distinctions are sometimes less obvious than they sound.

II

Economics is the study of wealth — its production, distribution, and consumption — with an eye to finding the practical consequences which follow from the nature of wealth itself.

In certain societies, where wealth is distributed by means of money, economics must include the study of monetary theory. But the primary subject is wealth, not money.

Economics helps to define what can or cannot be done, and to describe the probable consequences of the things which can be done. Economics does not help in the least to define what ought or ought not to be done. Among the many things which *can* be done in the economic order of any country at any moment in history, it is the moral problem to decide which of them *ought* to be done and the political problem to see to it that they *are* done. But when, as in our world, the moral purpose of society has become unsure, when there is no one way of life which is felt to be 'ordained' in the sense that it will give man the best chance to win salvation or to fulfill his nature, then the power of moral decision atrophies. There are no sure grounds on which to sort out what *should* be done from among the many courses which are economically possible.

When the power of moral decision declines, the strength and dignity of politics decline as well. Man is left alone with economics. But economics, when the burden of decision is put upon its shoulders, can only suggest which of the possible lines of conduct is likely to provide the most wealth. It cannot even do that accurately, for it is forced by its terms of reference to leave out of account the question of what man should be asked, or can be expected, to endure. For example, an economic order well adapted to maximizing the production of wealth might really prove 'uneconomic' if it were found necessary to keep a large and highly paid standing army in order to prevent the mass of the population from revolt. As soon as economics is asked to become a substitute for politics, it is degraded as a social science; and it never can become an adequate substitute.

III

Mr. Lionel Robbins, of the London School of Economics, is one of the men with the greatest insight into our perplexing economic order. His recent book, 'The Great Depression,'[1] is an important contribution to the literature of economics. At the same time (and this is no criticism of the book) it is a warning of the evil that must follow from setting economics above politics. In a chapter on 'Restrictionism and Planning' Mr. Robbins makes a grim attack on the idea that 'order' can be brought into finance-capitalism by giving each industry the right to restrict competition. The way in which such a policy of curtailment leads to bigger and bigger efforts at governmental 'planning,' and the way in which such 'planning' may lead first to tyranny and then to the destruction of capitalism in all its possible forms, is presented with deadly clarity.

'There is a snowball tendency about this kind of interventionism,' writes Mr. Robbins, 'which has no limit but complete control of all trade and industry. It is clear that, within the restricting industries, the State will be driven to adopt closer and closer control if the schemes are not to break down from evasion of their rules. It is one thing to forbid farmers and others to produce more than a certain quota. It is another thing to prevent their doing so. The Agricultural Adjustment Act which pays farmers to throw land out of cultivation contains the pathetic proviso that such restriction must be unaccompanied by "increase in commercial fertilization." How, short of the socialization of American farming, do the framers of this stipulation propose to put it into force?'

I do not believe that Mr. Robbins's argument can be upset.

[1] New York, 1934.

Yet I can think of nothing more unfortunate than that his book should be taken as a political, rather than an economic, treatise. For its political moral would be that the thing to do about America is nothing at all. Mr. Robbins is presenting the argument for *laissez-faire*, 'equilibrium' economics in its purest and most abstract form. In doing so he is performing a great service — but only if we regard his book as economics. So taken, it is an admirable way of pointing out the dangers of interfering with the economic machine. It is vital that we should understand those dangers. It is also vital that we should not delude ourselves into thinking we can leave the economic machine severely alone. We cannot leave it severely alone for *political* reasons, because man will not permit us to do so. This is something which economics can never teach us; it lies outside the realm of economic thought. If, therefore, in the present low estate of politics we seek to take economics as our sole guide, we shall learn many things not to do. And this is profitable knowledge. But you cannot run a great nation, in a time of world-crisis, solely by not doing things.

Another example of the same point can be found in Mr. Robbins's book. Discussing the American farm problem, Mr. Robbins comes to the following conclusions — all of which are 'sound economics': 'The difficulties of agriculture here, as elsewhere in modern economic history, are to be explained, in the large, in terms of an increase of productivity due to technical progress which encounters a relatively inelastic demand.... Technical progress in American agriculture has been very rapid. The American farmer is feeling with especial force the pressure of those influences which in the course of history have tended continually to reduce the proportion of effort devoted to the production of agricultural staples. In the beginning it was one hundred per cent. Since then it has been diminishing. In the absence of restriction, it would in all probability continue to diminish.'

The correct economic deduction from all this, says Mr. Robbins, is that 'a certain proportion of the producers of the products whose prices have fallen must change over to an occupation the demand for whose product is more elastic. There must be a reshuffling of the labor force — a contraction of the proportion employed on the production of products in relatively inelastic demand and an expansion of the proportion employed elsewhere.'

From the economic point of view this is complete. We must have fewer farmers. And if our technique of soil-culture improves, we must have still fewer farmers. And if the agrobiologists in Washington live up to their promises the time may come when a farmer is as rare as a dirigible balloon. The ex-farmers will be factory-hands, making products for which the demand is more 'elastic.' Perhaps they will be making pip-squeaks to put on the tables of night-clubs, or little celluloid dolls to hang in the rear windows of automobiles.

What about this program from the political point of view? To a communist it would sound more than gratifying. If there is one thing a communist dislikes, it is a farmer. If there is one thing he approves of, it is a factory-hand. It does not matter what the factory-hand is making, so long as he is a factory-hand, a proletarian, a man who has been prepared by his economic lot to receive the doctrine of Marx. But the very reasons which recommend this program to a communist make it distressing to a man who is interested in preserving the American experiment. If we dispossess millions of small proprietors, turning them into millions of proletarians, we shall have gone a long way toward making a self-governing nation of free men an impossibility within our borders. We shall have torn up the foundations of America, replacing them with foundations suitable for a fascist or a communist state.

All of this, however, is quite beside the point for Mr. Robbins. Economics is the study of wealth. It has nothing to do with the question of whether self-government is better than tyranny, free men better than slaves. Mr. Robbins has imagined a world in which there is a really free play of economic forces. He is pointing out that such a world will produce more goods, more wealth, if the economic forces are left entirely free, if they are never interfered with at any point. In the course of his argument he sheds much light on the way in which the existing economic order works, or fails to work. It is not his business to tell us what sort of world we want to live in. It is our business to decide that, on moral grounds. It is the function of politics to bring that desired world to life, after we have decided what it should be. It is the function of economics to tell us what we may expect, in regard to the production of wealth, from this, that, and the other policy. If, having no moral aim, we turn to economics as our sole counselor, it may very well guide us into a world capable of producing the maximum of goods; but we are duping ourselves if we expect it to guide us into a world where men will be content to live. A modern English historian has written that 'the free play of economic forces will invariably tend to a rich but never to a good society.' An understanding of the nature of economics will make it clear that this statement is a truism.

IV

In 'Religion and the Rise of Capitalism,' Mr. R. H. Tawney has written that the importance of the medieval view of economic problems lies in the 'insistence that society is a spiritual organism, not an economic machine, and that economic activity, which is one subordinate element within a vast and complex unity, requires to be controlled and repressed by reference to the moral ends for which it supplies the material means.' It is interesting to consider these two views of society — a 'spiritual organism,' and an 'economic machine' — with an eye to the vexed modern problem of 'planning.'

If society is a spiritual organism, then economics is subordinate to politics and both to morals. In that case we can have the sort of 'planned society' our American forefathers intended: a society based on moral principles that are clearly understood, a society in which the major institutions (such as self-government and widely diffused private property) are chosen and maintained because they are in keeping with the principles, a society with the freedom that only self-discipline can give. Planning, in these basic political-moral terms, is the purpose of statesmanship.

If we take the view that society is an economic machine, then we cannot attempt political or moral planning. A machine is a fixed thing; you cannot tamper with its nature. You can only see that it runs as smoothly as possible. In other words, the only planning such a society can attempt is economic planning. Politics comes down to a quarrel between the group that feels the machine will turn out more wealth if it is left entirely alone and the group that feels it will turn out more wealth if it is tinkered with from time to time. The result of this quarrel is often a compromise combining the worst features of the two methods: the machine is left alone whenever a question of moral interference might arise, but it is tinkered with just enough to spoil its economic efficiency.

The defeatism coloring so much of our feeling about politics is traceable to the widespread view that society is nothing but an economic machine. People feel we are caught in a system we cannot alter, that there is no use talking about the American dream, or about a society of free proprietors, or about any of the basic American ideas. All that is over and done with, because the machine will no longer permit it. And if it were true that economics comes first, these conclusions would logically follow. But it is not true — though it becomes true for all practical purposes if people persist in acting on the assumption.

Any economic system can be changed if its moral results are clearly understood and are felt to be displeasing — but the displeasure has to be sincere, not merely formal. It is a gross delusion to feel that the economic order has an independent existence. Back of economics lie morals. The morals of a society may be high or low, conscious or unconscious; but they cannot be non-existent. And the morals of a society determine what emotions will be allowed free play, what social conditions will be tolerated — they determine, in other words, the limits within which the economic system must move. In a world like ours, where people are unaccustomed to thinking in moral terms, the economic order can warp the morals of a society, can 'determine' them to a certain extent. But even in our world there is a last resistant set of moral assumptions which the economic order cannot change, to which the economic order must adjust itself.

For example, it has been economically desirable of late to close down many of the world's coal-mines. It would be equally desirable, economically, to close down the miners inside the mines so that they might not become a charge on the community. Yet the mines are closed, while the miners are kept partially alive. The reason for the inconsistency is a moral reason.

The more conscious a society is of its moral aims, the more aware it is of the relation between its aims and its actions, the less it will be economically 'determined,' the closer it will be to the ideal of a society as a 'spiritual organism' in which the economic order supplies the material means for the moral ends of life. Conversely, the more successful a society is in forgetting its moral ends, the more will economic determinism operate, the closer will society come to being an 'economic machine.' No society can be an economic machine pure and simple, for there is always a moral basis somewhere. And no society can become a spiritual organism pure and simple, for that would be perfection, and there will be no perfect social system previous to the appearance of perfect men. But between these two extremes the social order can vary infinitely. In the one direction it approaches a more and more unconscious, a more and more mechanical and determined state. In the other direction it approaches a state in which there is a noticeable relation between what society does in the economic sphere and what it feels to be right.

The importance of these distinctions in the world of action is that only by proceeding in the latter direction, only by ruthlessly subordinating economics to political and moral aims, can a nation hope to gain inner peace and self-esteem, and to give its citizens a way of life in which the plain man can know happiness and dignity. It is an ironic fact that the one group in the modern world which talks the most nonsense about economic determinism is the one group which makes no compromises when it comes to subjecting economic to moral considerations. I refer to the communists, whose chief strength is that they are politically and morally self-conscious.

Mr. Robbins can show that the free play of economic forces (which can only exist under a *régime* of the private ownership of the means of production) will produce more goods and services (more wealth) than will any form of controlled and planned economy. The communists take note of the information; they may make good use of it as they proceed with their plans; but it does not occur to them to submit to it, to permit the free play of economic forces. For their first aim is not to produce the greatest possible number of goods; their first aim is to build a world where the plain man can find justice. Those of us who dislike their picture of justice, who think their earthly paradise would be a hell, would do well to copy their steadfast moral purpose. For we can never combat such a purpose with a mere 'economic machine.' 'History,' writes Mr. Douglas Jerrold, 'affords no instance of a nation which subordinates politics to economics maintaining its position as a great power. The battle is to the politically conscious, not to the economically well-organized.' [1]

V

To sum up the distinctions I have sought to establish: First, the basic problem of statesmanship remains the moral problem. No society can long flourish unless its rulers (in a self-governing

[1] *England*, p. 220.

nation, its people) are agreed on the moral aims which are being sought. It must be accepted that a certain way of life is desirable, and that the purpose of the social order is to maximize the chance of attaining that way of life. If 'the maximum of production' is taken as the social aim, instead of 'a certain way of life,' the society is dying at its roots. Nations do not survive by accident. They survive because of moral qualities which give them inner strength. And no man's strength is as the strength of ten merely because his bank-account is growing. It has been written that 'there is no escape from the law which has made resolution, courage, audacity, an inspiration to sacrifice, and an exaltation in serving the condition of the enduring greatness of peoples.' None of these qualities can be provided by a mere economic machine. The America of the nineteen-twenties will serve as an abiding proof of that fact.

Second, the problem of politics is to adapt a troublesome and discordant world as closely as possible to the moral pattern which has been accepted. In doing this the economic welfare of the people must never for a moment be ignored. And it must never for a moment be taken as the sole aim.

Third, the problem of economics is to discover the effect of various political and moral environments on the production and distribution of wealth. The statesman sets the problem. We choose, he will say, for moral reasons, a nation with a majority of small proprietors, on the French or Danish model; or we choose a nation with no proprietors at all, but with State-directed production for use; or we choose a nation with a few big owners and many salaried workers, and with the State interfering to direct the relations between the two groups. We all know that each of these basic orders *can* work. We know that each of them produces its own characteristic moral environment, and its own political forms. The statesman, or his constituents, must choose the moral environment; there must be a conscious and active will of the people directed toward maintaining it; otherwise society will be an aimless flux. And great nations are not built by aimlessness. Given this basic choice, it is the function of economics to provide all the available facts as to what can be done to maximize the production of wealth. And at the same time economics should keep before the people the knowledge of what could be done under the other basic forms of society.

At the moment our literature offers surprisingly few examples of pure economics. One reason for this, I think, is that our aimless society is making a false demand upon the economists, which the economists are trying to meet. We are asking our economists to provide us with a substitute for a moral purpose. Unable, or unwilling, to give moral reasons for whatever social order we instinctively prefer, we are asking our economists to prove that the sort of world we should like to see is really the sort of world which would produce the most goods. That way madness lies — for the economists as well as for the rest of society.

It is significant that the men who are providing the nearest approach to dispassionate analyses are the economists of the extreme Right — the arch-conservatives who feel in their bones that whatever the political future holds it will not see again the world where their hearts dwell, that brief and partial *laissez-faire* world of nineteenth-century British practice. There is a wistful charm to the picture these men are giving of that Never-Never land of 'the free play of economic forces.' And there is an unrivaled accuracy and clarity to their descriptions of the experiments in control that are being carried on today. The work of Mr. Robbins, Dr. F. A. Hayek's 'Prices and Production,'[1] Mr. E. F. M. Durbin's 'Purchasing Power and Trade Depression'[2] — books like these contain the best of modern economic thought on the capitalist side. Because these men are not hopeful of becoming political advisers, they are able to do their business as economists with an accuracy that puts their opponents to shame. If we should demand from all our economists, not morals and not politics, but the most dispassionate analyses that the frail human mind can afford, the literature of economics would become a more impressive sight.

What we really demand is proof that communism, or finance-capitalism, or a 'planned' State capitalism, will make everybody rich. What we really get, therefore, is not economics but economic history. To explain what I mean by this phrase I must describe what I mean by history.

VI

History is one of the most natural forms of thought, yet it remains to this day one of the most obscure, one of the hardest to analyze. In my opinion Signor Croce's analysis is the most accurate that has yet been given. Croce begins by distinguishing between history and chronicle. Chronicle is the dead fact, the unrealized concept. When it is brought to life by an imaginative act, when the concept is illuminated by intuition, we have history. History and chronicle, writes Croce, are distinguishable 'as two different spiritual *attitudes*. History is living chronicle, chronicle is dead history.'

In bringing the dead chronicle back to life by means of his own intuitions, the historian is clearly likely to revive some-

[1] Second edition, London, 1935.   [2] London, 1933.

thing very different from what existed in the first instance. It is a precarious balance he is seeking, between concept and intuition, science and poetry. Leaving aside the question as to whether he ever attains this balance to perfection, it is worth noting that when he falls too far on the side of the concept, the chronicle, the result is what Signor Croce calls 'philological history,' which 'can certainly be *correct*, but not *true*.' And when the historian leans too far toward intuition the result is 'poetical history,' in which we find 'the substitution of the interest of *sentiment* for the lack of interest of thought, and of *aesthetic* coherence of representation for the logical coherence here unobtainable.... When life finds expression and representation before it has been dominated by thought, we have poetry, not history.' In other words, life and thought — document and criticism — are the two elements of the historical synthesis. When either is palpably overemphasized, we have a form of pseudo-history.

There is a third form of pseudo-history which is more common than the poetic or the philological. This third form is what Croce calls 'rhetorical history' — that is, history written to prove a point. Many of man's most interesting writings belong to this group. In the classical world there was a tendency to write history in order to show that the life of man moved in circles, returning upon itself with a regularity that justified the utmost pessimism. In the Middle Ages there was a tendency to write history to show that the Christian revelation introduced truth into the world, giving man his first fair chance to escape from classical pessimism. In the modern world there is a tendency to write history to show that one or another type of economic organization will give man a better chance to realize his hopes than he has ever had in the past. This is the sort of writing I referred to when I spoke of 'economic history.' It is interesting; it is illuminating; but it is not economics.

It is not economics because it has a moral aim. It is the attempt of a society which is losing its convictions, and therefore its basis for action, to find a new basis in a form of thought which does not lend itself to that use. Most of the Left Wing treatises of today belong to this category; for the Marxists, who have a true moral aim, are oddly ashamed of this advantage. They waste much effort in seeking to prove that they are merely embracing the 'economically inevitable.' People who have no moral aim, or who are ashamed of having one, always try to ally themselves with Destiny. For Destiny is impressive without being embarrassingly moral. Some of the most powerful and interesting of our contemporary books belong to this group — for example, Mr. John Strachey's 'The Nature of Capitalist Crisis,' and Mr. Lewis Corey's 'The Decline of American Capitalism.' It does not detract from their worth to suggest that they belong to the literature of moral exhortation rather than to the literature of economics. 'Das Kapital' itself is a curious combination of the two types. It contains a great deal of pure analysis, of magnificent fact-finding, which belongs to economics. And it contains a great deal of back-handed moralizing, which consists of asserting that Fate and all the dark powers of eternity are on the side of the Marxian dream.

VII

I have tried to suggest why the plain man finds the literature of economics confusing and unsatisfying. At the one extreme are the pure research problems, the statistical tables and abstract analyses which have nothing to do with the plain man. They are the necessary rock-bottom for economics, and they are properly written for the profession only. Then there is a small (far too small) group of books presenting in ordinary language, and with some impartiality, the main findings of economic science. Then there is the abundant literature of economic history, using the authoritative language and the magic catchwords to bolster up a moral thesis. It would be better for society if we could reach our moral conclusions on plain moral grounds, restricting our economic thought to the important field where it belongs.

THOMAS MANN

I incline to the view that only the exhaustive can be truly interesting.

KENNETH ROBERTS

The historical novelist's relation to research is practically the same as his relation to his wife.

LADY MURASAKI

But I have a theory of my own about what this art of the novel is and how it came into being. To begin with, it does not simply consist in the author's telling a story about the adventures of some other person. On the contrary, it happens because the story-teller's own experience of men and things, whether for good or ill — not only what he has passed through himself, but even events which he has only witnessed or been told of — has moved him to an emotion so passionate that he can no longer keep it shut up in his heart. Again and again something in his own life or in that around him will seem to the writer so important that he cannot bear to let it pass into oblivion. There must never come a time, he feels, when men do not know about it.

(Circa 1000)

MARGARET AYER BARNES
holds the opinion that it is fiction, and not history or biography, which preserves for posterity the temper of an age.

THE PERIOD NOVEL

THE phrase has come to have a vaguely archaic significance. It suggests plumed hats and rapiers, hooped skirts and powdered hair. Heroines who swoon and heroes who swagger. Stage-coaches, pillions, and sedan-chairs. It suggests, too, a book written in retrospect by a modern writer who cherishes a romantic or documentary interest in 'old, unhappy, far-off things.' Fiction does not seem 'period,' unless it mirrors the past.

And the past from the point of view of the present. We do not speak of Fielding's 'Tom Jones' or Fanny Burney's 'Evelina' as 'period novels.' Nor 'The Life and Opinions of Tristram Shandy, Gent.,' which served its author, Laurence Sterne, as a rambling vehicle in which to portray the manners and the morals of his time. The sub-title of the first edition of 'Clarissa' — 'The History of a Young Lady, Comprehending the Most Important Concerns of Private Life and Particularly Showing the Distresses that may attend the Misconduct of both Parents and Children in relation to Marriage' — reveals the interest of Richardson in problems that still touch us. It might have served John Galsworthy as a sub-title for the first great book of 'The Forsyte Saga,' 'The Man of Property.' The abundant life and energy that floods these fine old novels forbids us to classify them as romantic curiosities or antiquarian relics.

In the best sense of the word, however, fiction dealing with the contemporary scene is 'period' fiction. When well-written, it is authentic and will become historical: a page torn authoritatively from the book of the past. The writer knows what he is talking about, which is the first great asset of any chronicler. If he is observant and conscientious, he will tell the truth. Great art is, after all, only truth-telling. It is the honest recreation of life as the artist sees it. And the fact that it is *seen*, that in fiction it is coloured and enriched by the personal point of view of the author, gives a note of passionate and imaginative conviction to the portrayal that is lacking in the colder representation of biographer or historian.

What woman, in biography or even in autobiography, lives for us with the glowing simplicity and complete verisimilitude of Anna Karenina, as she emerged from Tolstoi's brain? What history depicts an age as Thackeray's 'Vanity Fair' depicts it? These questions define the tremendous opportunity and the fearful responsibility of the novelist.

For people read fiction, as they do not read histories and biographies. Continually, of course, descriptive or analytic volumes, written by scholars and statesmen and journalists, dealing with periods and personalities, have a popular vogue. They appear in 'best-seller' lists, vying with novels in the race to command the market. But, with rare exceptions, they do not live, as novels do, in the hearts and minds of the people. In the end it is the fiction that preserves for posterity the temper of an age. Trollope, Dickens, Thackeray, George Eliot, and the

Brontës have defined for us, forever, the one that was Victorian. Walter Scott and Jane Austen, as romanticist and realist, make the early nineteenth century live again.

Each novel, then, that is written, is essentially 'period.' If concerned with trivialities, in a few short years it will seem, as we say, to 'date.' Henry James's 'The Awkward Age' dates, for this reason, as such books as his 'What Maisie Knew' and 'The Ambassadors' will never be dated. The world has lost interest in the problem of the well-brought-up young girl, not brought up quite well enough to be ignorant of the social vices. Unfortunate Nanda was condemned by her contemporaries for the comparatively venal and certainly outmoded sin of having lost, psychologically, her maiden bloom. Her case is a plaintive one — no more. She cannot live with the pathetic, pulsing life of Maisie and Madame de Vionnet, whose lifelong tragedies and ephemeral joys spring from the eternal and honest conflict of the forces of good and evil.

So in writing a novel of manners, dealing with the present and the brief fragment of the past that lives in the memory of the writer, every conscientious novelist is doing period work. The great classic contemporary example is, of course, 'The Forsyte Saga,' which was recognized in the lifetime of its author as a social document of genius. Edith Wharton's 'The Age of Innocence' is, as its tender but somewhat condescending title implies, a slightly more self-conscious, though brilliantly executed, achievement of the same order. Willa Cather's 'A Lost Lady'— another tender title — which begins prosaically enough, 'Thirty or forty years ago, in one of those grey towns along the Burlington railroad...' and is primarily concerned with one woman's personal tragedy, competes with her books which deal more deliberately with definite historical characters, in delicately preserving 'the remembrance of things past.' Aldous Huxley's 'Point Counterpoint' sears London drawing-rooms with a pen as satiric, though far less good-humoured, than that of William Makepeace Thackeray. Arnold Bennett's 'The Old Wives' Tale' is the story of a generation. Victoria Sackville-West's 'The Edwardians' holds the transient glamour of an age we can still recall.

All honest craftsmen in the writer's trade consciously or unconsciously conserve this time-sense. Whether it is concerned with what happens today or what happened 'only yesterday,' it is a matter of fine perceptions and delicate adjustments. It is not easy to maintain. In dealing with precise chronological events, whether mental or factual, the first thing that impresses a writer is the startling inaccuracy of his own information about everything. He realizes at once that his fondest memory is not to be trusted, and that his deepest impression will bear corroboration.

What did people do and, above all, what did they think, at any given time? What they did can be reconstructed by reading books of contemporary reference, consulting the files of newspapers and talking with observant friends. A mistake, no matter how slight, is invariably called to the writer's attention, within a week of publication, by a score of readers. For nothing, apparently, so delights a reader as to discover and correct an inaccuracy on the printed page.

These corrections are welcome, however, as errors can be rectified in subsequent editions. And the writer knows, hearteningly, that they were made only because he succeeded in awakening in the minds of his fellow beings an exact and nostalgic memory of their own immediate past.

But music, words of song, details of dress and custom, and

the joyous vernacular of slang must all be dated before they are woven into the warp and woof of a story. A novelist of manners, delving into the past forty years of American living, can make of this research an amusing parlour game. He is received with cheers, when he asks — Just when was the vogue of Charles Dana Gibson? Who wrote 'David Harum'? When did you last dance the 'Boston' — the 'grapevine' — the 'maxixe' — the 'tango' and the 'Castle walk'? When did you sing 'Daisy Bell' — 'The Rosary' — 'In the Good Old Summer Time' — 'Tammany' — the 'Merry Widow Waltz' — 'Poor Butterfly' — and 'Put Your Head Down, Fritzy Boy'? When did you first hear the telling words, 'She pets'? When did 'petting' change to 'necking'? When did the hemline of an evening gown first rise above the feminine kneecap? When did it drop dramatically to the ankle with the advent of Lanvin's 'robe de style'? At what period of our social history were cocktails served unobtrusively to men in the dressing-room, lest the lips of some reckless lady be defiled by hard liquor? When were you first startled to see the end of a cigarette stained red with lipstick? When did you last disapprove of a woman who powdered her nose in public? When were ankles hobbled, arms bared, skirts slit, hatpins discarded, and corsets abandoned? When did a lady first show her thigh with impunity on a public bathing-beach? When did your car have its first self-starter? When were acetylene headlights outmoded? When did bicycles 'scorch'?

Trivial questions — but upon them, and others like them, depends the authenticity of the time-sense. And upon them, too, depend, to a great extent, the manners and morals of a given age. For our social customs spring from our mental content, and our mental content, in turn, is influenced by our social customs. It is a vicious, or a virtuous, circle, as the case may be, depending upon the trend of the times.

For the important events of our recent history — as well as for many a side-light upon the lesser ones — the files of the newspapers are the great resource of the writer. They preserve the opinion of the moment, like a fly in amber. And the opinion of the moment is often of a nature to awaken both pity and terror — and mirth, as well — in the heart of the reader detached from it by even a brief period of time.

But in reading those files, the deepest impression received is that of the great resilience of human nature. The headlines cry of calamity down the years — for calamity is so often news. Waves of war and graft and speculation and depression break over the human race — break and recede and break again — but they leave the human race incredibly and stoically the same. For comfort and consolation you must turn to the back pages of the newspapers. There, while empires fall and civilizations crumble, the Cubs and the Sox are battling for the pennant; Min and Andy are pursuing the adventure of domesticity; women are being informed how to win their lovers, hold their husbands, discipline their children, make bread pudding, and that this is a velvet season. In the back pages of the newspapers, as in the back streets of the cities, surrounded by apparent trivialities, you find human nature running true to form, carrying on with amazing indifference and stupendous courage in the face of catastrophe.

'As people feel life, so will they feel the art that is most closely related to it.' Henry James said that, in his essay on 'The Art of Fiction.' It explains, I think, the eternal popularity of the novel form. The fact, too, that the novels that endure are those, by and large, whose theme is rooted, subtly perhaps, but sincerely, in the conflict of moral forces.

It throws some light, as well, on the ephemeral popularity of the 'best-seller.' It makes you understand what may be the common denominator in the very divergent output of, let us say, Kathleen Norris and Willa Cather, Harold Bell Wright and Thornton Wilder. James Hilton, too, who flashed into fame with 'Goodbye, Mr. Chips,' and 'The Lost Horizon.' And Victoria Lincoln, the young author of 'February Hill,' which, in spite of its modern cast of prostitutes, drunks, and rum-runners, is nothing more nor less than the 'Mrs. Wiggs of the Cabbage Patch' of this generation. Different as these writers may be from the point of view of artistry, they all believe, quite simply and sincerely, in being good.

Virtue is as realistic as vice. The average reader likes to perceive in the pattern of a plot the shadowy design of his own personal problems. And one thing is certain — that men and women in every age believe some things to be good and others to be bad, and try, with indifferent success in the perplexity of living, to differentiate between them. It is the task of the writer to interpret that effort, to portray the heliotropic struggle of humanity in the jungle of existence to reach the sun.

H. G. WELLS

An autobiography is the story of the contacts of a mind and a world.

GAMALIEL BRADFORD

Biography is the study of you and me.

EMILY DICKINSON

If I read a book and it makes my whole body so cold no fire can ever warm me, I know that it is poetry.

DAVID McCORD

The only anthology of the slightest use whatever is the kind we carry about in our heads.

BEN RAY REDMAN

A book is a new book if you haven't read it.

WILLIAM HAZLITT

I cannot understand the rage manifested by the greater part of the world for reading new books.

ESTHER FORBES differentiates between novels of romantic color, those which mirror a past age, and others dealing with the constancy of human nature.

WHY THE PAST?

'BUT will you always lay the scenes of your stories in the past?' she asked me, a little pityingly.

'I rather think so.'

It was back in the twenties when the amateur psychoanalyst was rather more to the fore than today. I might have guessed her next remark.

'There must be something in the present that you cannot face. For some reason you cannot cope with reality.'

'I do not think that is the reason, but...'

'The need for a more romantic world shows a frustration by the world you live in. And that,' she added triumphantly, 'is the reason why people both read and write novels of other periods than their own. It is an attempt to escape reality.'

I knew that if I showed the irritation which I felt she would have proof that she was right. That was the trouble with the amateur psychoanalyst. If you agreed, they won. If you did not, they won. For you, it was always a losing battle.

After she was gone I tried to think things out. Like many

people I think best with a pencil in my hand. So today I can open a notebook and read at the top of a blank page:

'Jan '27. Why the past?

'1) Escape from reality; into a more beautiful or at least more exciting world than the one we actually know.'

I judge by the look of the page I must have spent some time on the subject. Everything has been underlined. There are boxes about the words 'escape,' 'reality,' and 'past.' From these boxes delicate tendrils emerge. The tendrils are trimmed with dots. All this, of course, represents intense thought. Nor does one draw three cartwheels and an elaborate scalloped edging in a moment. Looking at that page today I must believe it represents at least an hour's 'work.'

And I had left the rest of the page blank, showing that I had hoped to go back to it and add other reasons besides the frustration motive that had so irritated me.

The page has remained blank for eight years.

Once again the notebook; this time without irritation.

'June '35.

'Why the Past?

'1) Something in what M. P. s'd. Natural craving of man for more romantic world. (Nothing to be ashamed of.) Always have been "giants in those days." "Strange beauty" (see editorial of Bolitho's). But has its bad side. Gives license to situations that would seem thin or improbable if told with contemp. background. License for characters often too ideally bad or good. Reader not so critical of character and action of an early age. Writers of historical romances often take too much license. Note. In Victorian America more license *in re* nakedness &

vice. Editors wouldn't stand either except with hist. setting. Writer could pave streets of Rome with most seduct. & flamboy. courtesans but never (Stephen Crane) picture contemp. harlot. Same true art. Bouguereau's nymphs. Powers' Greek Slave. Manet's less naked but contemp. "Déjeuner sur l'Herbe" howled down...'

But the digression is running away with the page. And surely no one today is being driven to write of ancient Rome because he wishes license of that sort. 'There's Popeye,' I thought, 'and Mr. Faulkner. I wonder if seventy-five years ago Mr. Faulkner would have been forced by public opinion to shroud him with a toga?'

So far we have only said that novels of the past are written (1) to escape from the heavy gray world of our reality into a more golden day. Homer fulfilled this need for his contemporaries. Scott, Dumas, Lytton for theirs. Sabatini, Cather, Hergesheimer, Feuchtwanger, Undset for ours. Shakespeare, Thackeray, Thomas Mann, Tolstoy...

Now it is time to stop in confusion. Make more cart wheels. Draw boxes, tendrils, and dots. A yard or two of scalloped edging. These names grouped together begin to make no sense at all.

It is true that all of these writers have set much of their best work in the past. But you can't just lump them together. Say they were all flying South to more halcyon shores like migrating swallows. All 'escaping reality.' 'Not "War and Peace,"' I thought. 'Why did Tolstoy choose the period of his father and grandfather for his greatest novel rather than the Russia of his own day? For some reason he found greater "reality" in the past than in the present.'

So beside the highly romantic, frankly 'escape' novels such as Dumas, Scott, Sabatini (and I rather think Homer as well), there is emerging...

> '2) Novels laid in the past, not to escape reality, but to increase it. The actual unchanging human animal with his soul and his other problems seen more clearly through the perspective of time. (*Why?*)'

And there should be a third group to include those novels written by men who are primarily historians. The period itself in a way because the most carefully studied character — So —

> '3) Novels dominated by their own epochs.'

Now that there are three divisions it is interesting (but idle) to try to fit old friends into their proper holes. Scott and Sabatini and Hervey Allen's 'Anthony Adverse' all at first sight seem to belong in Number 1. They all have glamour aplenty and the pages are strewn thicker with fair ladies and gallant men than life as I know it. And there is more and prettier coincidence. If a lady falls off her horse into your arms in Worcester, Massachusetts, in the year 1935, the chances are that, instead of being the loveliest creature you ever saw, riding to save the life of a king, she will turn out to be a friend of your mother's who has taken up equestrianism for the sake of her figure. But not with Messrs. Scott and Dumas, Sabatini and Allen. And yet all of these writers have something of Number 3 in them. They have based their work on careful scholarship. Well-known names and battles are carefully pictured. Allen, at least, has gone one step farther. I think he tried to show (even as Walpole in 'Fortitude') the unbreakable spirit of man. He wanted Anthony, the human being, to emerge and dominate the flying coaches, the slave marts, the ships. But Anthony, the human being, went down under the romantic trappings. 'No,' I thought, 'you belong in Number 1, with a little of Number 3 in you and an attempt at Number 2.'

Shakespeare seems to me about equally divided between Number 1 and Number 2, but is very innocent of Number 3. 'Kristin Lavransdatter' is a perfect example of all three groups equally merged — romantic color, human nature, the picture of a past age. Feuchtwanger is almost pure Number 3.

'War and Peace,' 'Vanity Fair,' 'Wuthering Heights,' 'The Old Wives' Tale' — these names bring up another point, and that is the incredible number of great books that have been written, not of the far-past, but of the just-past, the age of one's father, one's grandparents. Most of these I think belong primarily in Number 2. There must be something very stimulating in the haze that exists between the author's maturity and the time his parents or grandparents were young and he himself unborn. The fathers of both Thackeray and Tolstoy were young men when Napoleon fought his wars. Why did their sons choose this period for their greatest novels? 'Wuthering Heights' ends in 1802. Emily Brontë was born in 1818. I had read 'Wuthering Heights' two or three times before I realized that it was not of Emily's own contemporaries that I was reading. Not even of her own century, for most of the action takes place long before 1800.

It needs but a few generations before the casual reader loses track of the chronological relationship between the novels of the 'just-past' and their writers. One could easily imagine that 'Jonathan Wild' was a cut-throat of Fielding's own period, a piece of observation as contemporary to its author as 'Main

Street' or 'Babbitt' is to Sinclair Lewis. But the Great Mr. Wild was born some forty years before his creator. If he had lived to be an old scamp, Fielding might have met him in his own court, but he was hanged young.

'The Old Wives' Tale.' I am sure that many college seniors reading this book for a course on the English novel will take it for granted that Bennett reported what he himself had seen. This is far from the truth. It is only when Constance and Sophia were middle-aged or old women that Bennett could have known them. The siege of Paris that he describes so plausibly — he was three years old at the time and could not even have read of it in newspapers.

'Buddenbrooks.' Thomas Mann was a young man when he wrote this book. He, like Bennett, might have known his heroine as an ageing woman. But he went far back before the period of his own actual observation to create Toni, the child, the young girl, the matron; and the old-fashioned world she lived in.

Endless books, and some of them the best that we have, belong to this 'just-past' group. And we must all have noticed that often the beginning of some very ordinary novel is convincing and good. That part about how the parents meet or the grandparents moved into this valley and began to lay out a farm. The hero and heroine as children. This seems very well done. But as soon as the story catches up with the present, it struggles, gasps, is seen awry and without clarity. It is confused. Something has been lost. Something which for a chapter or two the writer actually had. You throw the book down. It is another of these books that 'peter out.'

There must be some reason why so many writers from the greatest to the least can find more freedom to tell a story and observe the men and women of their creation in some other period than their own. It does not need to be very far back. As I have said, one's parents' and grandparents' day seem to be the most fruitful. Why are those years, roughly thirty to fifty years before one's own, so stimulating?

There is normally (we are told) a slight warfare between the crowding younger generation and the one just preceding it. No furniture (each generation thinks) is quite as ugly as that of one's parents. No ideas or ideals quite so stale. This youthful state of mind is accepted as necessary to get the young ego upon its own feet. Then why do so many of these young egos when they start to write do their best work in this theoretically damned just-past age? Having thought of this puzzle to the extent of several cart wheels, I must admit it is a problem for the psychiatrist rather than for me. Still there is no reason why I should not have my own ideas on the subject.

The first past-age a child struggles to re-create realistically is that of his parents or, if he has contact with them, of his grandparents. The stories of Robin Hood and the Sleeping Princess are his escape to romance. This is the dream-world where anything may happen. When he grows up it is that part of him which demands the romantic novel of escape. But his reaction to the stories of his mother or grandmother is slightly different. 'When I was a little girl my father — your great-grandfather — planted all those trees at the foot of the lawn. He told me not to step on them, but I rolled my hoop over them and broke the top off that black walnut.' Here is a curious adjustment for a child to make. Once not only were those great trees so little a child could step on them, but your grandmother was little too and she rolled a hoop instead of (like yourself) developing spinal curves with a scooter-bike.

And your father used to ride his pony over country roads which now (widened to forty feet) roar with traffic. Even if you had a pony there would be no place to ride it. The automobiles have devoured that entrancing way of life. These old days seem golden and idyllic, unreal and yet perhaps more real than one's own world. The child can almost put out his hand to grasp this vanished day. Years later, when he sits down to write, all these early impressions come back with nostalgic clarity. This old way of life has simplicity, dignity. It already has that slight removal that is the basis of so much of the best fiction.

It is not true that all writers have the need to hold their material away from themselves. Many have succeeded by reporting exactly what they have seen. But others must build up in some way a slight insulation between themselves and the material they are using, before the story gains its own independence. Too close contact warps the story, makes it seem unreal. To be actually 'seen,' it must be pushed away from oneself. It is a little like the feeling you sometimes may have on seeing someone dear to you when he is unconscious of your presence. A sudden awareness of the person, not as part of your life, but as an utterly separated entity. For instance, a man on a Fifth Avenue bus looks down and sees his wife standing on the crowded sidewalk. She does not see him. He knows her with a sudden flash of intuition. From behind the windshield of your sedan you see your father patiently waiting to cross the traffic of a busy street. He is an old man. You had not known it before. And all this automobile traffic is rather a new problem to him. You see him and the massed cars in new perspective. Before entering her own house, a woman glances in through a window. That is her son sprawled on the floor studying an atlas. The room is dark except for the light on his book and the top of his head. He is alone in the empty house. It is almost as though he were alone in the world, and the woman has a realization of this child, not as her 'baby,' but as the inherently lonely human being which each of us is.

For a moment these people have not been observed as 'my wife,' 'my father,' 'my son.' The ego of the observer has been withdrawn. They are themselves. In such a way the ego of the author is obliterated by pushing his characters farther away from himself — back perhaps into a time when he himself was unborn. He has them at arm's length. They are no longer 'my wife,' 'my father,' 'my son,' but Mary, Mr. Dickenson, and George. Now he can see them, understand them, and perhaps forgive them as he could not the sharers of his roof and personal problems. The character is liberated to be herself or himself and is not accountable to the author's hurt feelings, boredom, vanity, love, or jealousy.

In this way the novel of the past is 'an escape from reality,' for the realest thing, the final reality to each person, is himself, and yet many must make this escape from themselves before they can gain a proper perspective for their work.

Many stories are laid in the past because to each generation his own age must seem very complicated and to be filled with events which one does not know how to ignore and which have no value in themselves either to the situations or to the characters of the story. He cannot see the forest for the trees. When I began my first novel, the World War had been over only seven or eight years. Any character I put into a book would have (so it seemed to me) to account for those war years. But how? I did not feel capable of taking any hero to France and back again. And then at that time (the time of 'Flaming

Youth' and Scott Fitzgerald) so much was being said about the 'modern girl.' Every book in which she appeared seemed one more attack upon her or one more defense. I had less than nothing to say on that subject — having an idea that human nature is always about the same. I set the scene of my story back about seventy-five years and so believed I had escaped the War and escaped the flapper and might tell my story undisturbed. Not entirely. The reviewers avidly pointed out the fact that my genteel young lady — in spite of hoop skirts and a propensity to blush — was a 'flapper of the eighteen-fifties.' Perhaps she was. As I say, human nature does not change very much. But by using a period remote from myself I had gained a certain freedom from the loud talk of the moment. I had placed this girl far enough away from me so that I could see her as a human being — not merely as a modern young person.

'A Mirror for Witches' was the outcome of an interest, common among the younger writers of the twenties, in psychology — especially morbid psychology. Why then did I feel the need of putting my pathological specimen back into the seventeenth century? Why was it more interesting to me to explain how a neurotic girl of that distant period came to believe herself a witch than why some neurotic fellow dweller in Greenwich Village developed a phobia in regard to subway trains? One idea was exciting, the other boring. I wanted the dark color of Salem and Essex County. In my notebook I see I have set down the wish to write 'something of a fairy story for adults, explained by modern psychology, but having the same wonder and strangeness a child gets from Lang or Grimm.' If it was a fairy story I was trying to write, the claustrophobic lady of Greenwich Village would have been hard to handle.

In 'Miss Marvel,' the action begins two years after the Civil War and ends in 1933. Therefore it covers all but two years of my own life and many more besides. In writing this novel I did not gag once over the War — which had seemed so formidable to me ten years before. In those ten years something had happened to me. I had digested events which at the time seemed too chaotic. Now the War is definitely a thing of the past and for me therefore fluid and usable. I had to look up in the Britannica to find out what was going on in May, 1915. Perhaps it is not until great events have had time to find their places in encyclopedias that they actually become material for the novelist. Surely the best books of the War came out many years after the fighting was over. And it took a generation or two to produce the great novel on Napoleon's Russian campaign. It may be some child, who today is listening to the stories of his father's army life in France and feeling a queer nostalgic pull toward those fascinating days before he was born, who will write the 'War and Peace' of our generation.

MARY AUSTIN

Literary ability and intelligence do not necessarily grow on the same tree.

HARRIET MONROE

A masterpiece is no isolated miracle but a conspiracy between a man of genius and an epoch.

CLEMENCE DANE

The reader and writer are one flesh: and of their union the living book is born.

EDITH WHARTON

It is obvious that a mediocre book is always too long and that a great one usually seems too short.

AGNES REPPLIER

A book has a separate message for every reader, and tells him, of good or evil, that which he is able to hear.

DOROTHY THOMPSON

The adumbrations of surrounding life strike upon the sensitive instrument of the poetic mind and guide its production; what is produced, however, is not a phonograph record, but a new music.

E. ARNOT ROBERTSON
sees a book as the product of leisure and character, the focus of a mass of incompatible emotions.

ON ANSWERING QUESTIONS

LEISURE and character: these, apparently, are the main qualifications for the pursuit of letters, in the opinion of those not engaged in that pursuit. The proof of this is that the two questions most frequently asked of authors are: 'I've always meant to have a shot at writing a book myself, but somehow I've never found time; however do you manage it?' and: 'Isn't it awfully hard to keep yourself at it; I could imagine starting a book, but I'd never have the energy to go on to the end?'

As far as I can make out, all authors without exception are asked these two questions at varying intervals, whether they are detective fiction kings or obscure producers of mathematical treatises. There are roughly three classes of authors: the 'born-author' type, who is the person generally meant when the word 'writer' is used vaguely; he is mentally incapable of doing anything else and quite unable not to write, even if publication were impossible and he could only keep a diary. Then there is the honest craftsman who would just as soon be a stockbroker or a hotel-keeper if he could get as pleasant a living that way, but wants to do his job decently all the same. And there is the hack-writer who does not care what he writes as long as he gets the money.

I should say at a guess that about a quarter of the people earning their living as novelists are 'born authors,' which does not mean that they are born good authors: some remain bad all their lives, worse than most of those who competently follow the trade for a living. But the 'born author' is the one to whom life is an opportunity for writing rather than writing a means of living: he may never be able to translate effectively into words all the nebulous ideas in his head; but they, not what happens in his outer life, are the real centre of his interest; and while his heart can be broken by mundane events as easily as the next man's, even when he is at the deepest levels of misery one part of his mind is standing apart and saying, 'Now do try to remember that this is how a man feels when his heart is broken.' The 'born author' cannot understand the more impersonal attitude to work taken up by the honest craftsman, who in turn cannot understand him; and neither can have any sympathy, save superficially, with the hack-writer. But all three are required to think out suitably self-deprecatory replies to those strange recurrent compliments on their enviable idleness and their endurance.

These two questions seem to mark the beginning and the end of lay curiosity about the craft of letters, if one except the other but far rarer query as to whether the author uses a dictaphone, or a typewriter, or dictates to somebody, or writes it all out by hand himself. But if it is limited, this curiosity is at any rate universal: in four continents, now, I have struggled to find something courteous and at the same time not too blatantly idiotic to say in reply to these inquiries; and I have, of course, failed, because if one is hampered by politeness or any regard for truth, there is no possible reply that will not make one sound either conceited or a fool. If I have not yet failed in the fifth continent to explain why writers write it is because I have not yet had the chance of seeing Australia: others, more fortunate in the way of travelling, report that there, too, the interest in these two aspects of authorship is just the same and just as exclusive of any other interest as it is in Europe, America, Asia, and Africa. Odd.

Very occasionally — say once to every ten of either of the two standard questions — there crops up, 'Do you wait for your ideas to come to you, or do you work regular hours?' but this is really a variant of the leisure question: as long as a writer has time to do either, lucky devil, it is assumed that inspiration must follow.

Why is it that, while practically nobody knows or cares how books get themselves written, practically everyone feels competent to lay down the law on their value? — 'Wodehouse's stuff is much Better than Sapper's; he's got Style.' — 'Darling, he hasn't, he's Funny.' — 'I know, but you can be Funny and have Style; at least Wodehouse can. That's why he's so much Better.' — This I overheard in a lending library: neither of the speakers would have felt equal to passing an opinion on the proportions of a drawing, and if they had been asked whether they liked the appearance of a house they would probably have looked blank, yet they certainly went into more houses than they read books, and what with advertisement hoardings, and snaps taken of and by themselves, and the illustrations in fashion papers, they must also have seen more pictorial art than art of any other kind.

It is not familiarity, then, that leads people automatically to believe themselves authorities on books though on no other branch of creative work, but, I believe, the general idea that whereas a sculptor works under incomprehensible stresses of pure intellect and aesthetic passion, the writer, unless he is an exceptionally serious person, is working only to amuse or interest or at best both. And as the reader can easily tell whether he is amused or interested, he can equally easily tell whether the book is a good book or not, even without the help of 'style,' which makes the funny bits funnier and the rest more pleasing, so that naturally writers have it when they can, like the fortunate Mr. Wodehouse.

This attitude of non-familiarity-bred contempt for written art, as against other kinds, is summed up in the saying, 'Talks like a book.' That always means that the person described talks ponderously, flowerily or insincerely, and therefore badly. The only man I ever met who actually said 'Heigh-ho' when things went wrong was very much insulted when the phrase was applied to him, though his idea of apposite expressions must have come from his reading, and I suspect that the one thing which deterred him from saying 'Pshaw' in answer to the charge was that whereas 'Heigh-ho' is fairly obviously pronounced 'Hay-hoe,' 'pshaw' is a bit tricky.

With the tiny minority of writers whom the public recognises as serious it is assumed, on the grounds of their efforts to keep their character convincing, that they are only trying to produce something which can be called 'True to life'; and it is also assumed — on what grounds I do not know — that every reader knows all about life, so that even the serious writers present no difficulties of judgment to people who would hesitate to say whether they thought a poster a jumble of crude colours, or a particular bird's song musical.

The balance of rather ill-concealed contempt which most readers and most writers really feel for one another — apparently heaviest on the reader's side — is really levelled up by the inevitable egotism of authors, who could not write at all, I believe, if each of them were not — the 'born authors' anyway — two quite different people when planning and discussing work and when actually doing it.

Thinking of it in advance, they are generally as humble as the low esteem in which they are held by readers can possibly make them: they reflect with grateful astonishment that the lucky sale of the last book will keep them going nicely for a year and a half, so that they need not hurry with the next; they wonder how soon they can afford to experiment with that rather unpopular theme which they have long been yearning to try out in a novel: or else they are repulsively truculent, laying down the law on Trends In Modern Literature to anyone who will listen, and they may even be led on to dreadful remarks on What My Public Expects, and What I Intend to Give It: in either case the reader is in full view.

But when they finally get down to work, and stop drawing windmills and faces over the embarrassingly clean scribbling block on which most new books begin (I know of nothing more paralysing to the imagination than a new writing pad that is waiting to be filled) the reader fades out suddenly, and with a completeness which would astonish this proud person. Financial considerations fall away, the unpopular theme becomes the only one that is not entirely pointless here and now, its unpopularity becomes, indeed, an aspect too trivial to notice; and if any born writer were capable of remembering the existence of other writers while in the midst of the excitement, despondency and preoccupation of starting a new book, it would be only to wonder pityingly how they got along without this enchanting subject as a stimulus and companion. To the writer at work the reader — any reader but the private one sitting at the back of his brain who alone must be satisfied — is nothing but a gratifying and profitable irrelevancy.

Between spells of work, the doubts and hopes of success and understanding come back, but only in between. If an author remembers that last successful book while he is in his writing self, it is not with gratitude or truculence towards those peculiar strangers, its purchasers, but with mild speculation as to what the misguided people thought they saw in it to make them buy it, since no one could possibly understand the really important things about it except the person for whom it was written, its creator.

This is why the standard questions are so awkward for the author to answer: he cannot explain all this in reply to a query prompted half by such oddly bounded curiosity and half by the tacit assumption that he is a funny person probably unable to discuss golf, politics or other normal topics with ease, so that in kindness the non-writers must come on to his ground. Wondering how a writer makes time to write seems to him a little like asking however he found the leisure to cut his first teeth, or by what means an epileptic gets a minute to spare in which to have a fit: writing, like these things, just happens to the born writer and takes whatever time it wants out of his life. And the second stock question — the one about getting to the end of a book in which he is living, while he writes, more vividly than in his real surroundings — this is like asking a diver who has just left the high diving board head downwards how he persists in his descent until he reaches the water.

All of which makes it plain, I hope, that it is impossible to answer the question: 'What is a book?' for a book is bound to be a totally different thing to different people, particularly to those classes most interested in it, the three types of writer, and the reader. To most readers, I gather, it is a more or less competent piece of work which they might have done themselves given enough of the primary ingredients, leisure and character. To the hack writer it is a financial tight-rope feat — how much pornography can he balance across a line of luscious sentimentality? To the honest craftsman it represents a quiet gamble on the intellectual stock market; he invests a certain amount of mental sweat in his belief that the public will welcome a picture of the private life of a taxi-driver or the seamy side of the Italian pension business, but having decided where to try for his dividends he will probably put a great deal of quite unnoticeable conscientious work into polishing up minor characters to please himself, and in contriving situations that satisfy his sense of reality, not only the public's. And to the 'born author,' if the book is his own, it is the focus of a mass of incompatible emotions.

He struggles with the certainty that no one had a better idea, that no one ever handled a good thing worse. That on the other hand there are bits of it which express almost what he intended to say, and send a glow of exultation through him whenever he remembers them (say two paragraphs of about three hundred words each, in a novel of ninety thousand words). That no one but himself ought to be allowed to read it because no one else can see it as it was meant to be, not as it is. That everyone ought to be made to read it because of Chapter Two. That he wishes he could rewrite Chapter Two, because it throws the rest out of proportion. That he wishes he had not finished it, because to be bereaved of work on it is like losing a close friend.

That he hopes never to be reminded, by further sight or hearing of it, that he has failed again in the artist's job of recording only what he sees to be true, and has fallen into the shame of writing what he would merely like to be true, and nothing else matters but this. (Incidentally nothing *does* matter but this: I believe that whether he expresses it to himself in this way or not, all writers who aren't hacks subscribe to the same belief: That there is nothing intrinsically right or wrong but this, which is wrong: to let one's artistic judgment be swayed by one's personal wishes. A writer's duty is to be an unbiassed umpire watching the game of life, and whatever the mysterious sin against the Holy Ghost may be for other people, for him it is to suggest in his work that anything he has observed, love or death or ambition or sorrow, is nobler or sillier or more enduring or less important than he really believes it to be.)

The 'born author' worries miserably about his work, the craftsman worries a bit and the hack does not worry at all. In the circumstances the astonishing thing is not that there are a good many unscrupulous writers who deliberately write down to the lowest public, but that on the whole there are so few who produce shoddy stuff merely because they cannot be bothered to do better. This is all the more surprising when one realizes that far greater profits may be expected from a book called, say, 'My Blood, My Milk and My Tears,' with every page oozing some of this stimulating mixture, than from perhaps a dozen painstaking but utterly uninspired studies of adolescent love in a small town, dull as the life described. Yet literally hundreds of the latter are written every year, including the dozens that eventually find their way into publication, by people badly in need of the money to be made by following the prescription as above. They may have no hope of getting anywhere in their present line, but their artistic conscience functions better than their creative urge, and they will not offend it. Authors, particularly socially, are not an attractive lot: they are apt to be assertive, or self-conscious, or unpleasing to the eye, but taken as a whole from the moral point of view they are — whether they are craftsmen or born authors — extremely respectable, to use those poor words 'moral' and 'respectable' in their important sense for once.

Really that is one of the most interesting things about the writing trade, the conscientiousness which shows through nine out of ten books even when, as books, they are poor things. The unforgivable thing for any fiction writer to do is, as suggested before, to betray his own observation of life, in order to please the vast public who are not concerned with probabilities but enjoy reading by 'the light that never was on land or sea' — a bad light either to write or read by: but one has to accept the fact that most readers want from a book a means of escape from reality. And yet at the price of being rather boring, which most books are to that public which can reward so lavishly when given its escape, authors keep pretty constantly before them the unfortunate fact that truth has got to be stranger than fiction, otherwise it is unsatisfactory fiction. When, as frequently happens, they fall into romantic and too-highly coloured error it is, quite obviously, a genuine mistake in most cases.

Perhaps it is because the author, for the sake of his work, has to spend so much time looking into his own mind that he dares not risk finding there deliberate intellectual dishonesty, the most depressing of all self-discoveries. This may account for his surprising goodness in just that one respect, or it may be the natural stiffness of moral fibre demanded by a trade that can be followed at irregular hours and has no fixed rules, so that there is nothing to stop him knocking off for the day at any moment, and relegating everything to a tomorrow that never comes.

The unpleasant conclusion from the last paragraph is that a writer really does depend on our two old friends, time for introspection, and persistence in using it, in order to get his work done. Horrible thought, perhaps the public is right, and that is what a book really is, the product of leisure and character.

MICHELANGELO

The more the marble wastes, the more the statue grows.

HERVEY ALLEN

My trouble in writing is not to find material to put in but to dig around and find the things that can be left out.

THOMAS WOLFE

A novel is a trunkful.

CHEKOV

When you have written a story strike out both the beginning and the end. That is where we novelists are most inclined to lie.

JOHN GALSWORTHY

A good novel like a successful author is well rounded in the middle and skimpy at both ends.

HENRY SEIDEL CANBY

Ninety-nine long modern novels out of a hundred could be cut from one-quarter to one-third with positive gain.

JAMES NORMAN HALL,
*from the perspective of Tahiti,
examines one of the noblest
diseases of the human spirit.*

CACOËTHES SCRIBENDI

ACCORDING to the lexicographers, *cacoëthes* is an ill habit, or the itch for doing something inadvisable; and they add, 'as in *scribendi cacoëthes*, scribbling mania.' Why is this the customary illustration? Why have these words been so long and so intimately associated? Dictionaries are social as well as etymological histories, summing up briefly the garnered wisdom of the ages upon innumerable subjects, and the deduction in this case is that the itch for writing has always been regarded, not only as an affliction, but as the most contagious and prevalent of afflictions.

Nevertheless, it seems to me that 'itch,' 'mania,' 'ill habit,' are misleading terms, by no means descriptive of a malady which, in its higher manifestations, is one of the noblest diseases of the human spirit. Now and then, to be sure, even an illustrious victim speaks of it as though it were, in truth, nothing more than a disgusting irritation, something to be ashamed of. Tolstoy, for example, in a letter written in mid-course of his career, said: 'I abstain from writing and feel a kind of moral purity, such as one feels from not smoking. I do not know how to rejoice sufficiently at having conquered that habit.' But I doubt whether Tolstoy were as content and easy in mind as he professed to be at the moment. If he abstained from writing, the reason was, more than likely, that inspiration had failed him, temporarily, and he was trying to make a virtue of necessity. Had he been permanently cured, I venture to say that, thenceforth, he would have been the most miserable of men.

For a remarkable feature of the disease, and one of the most difficult to explain, is that, however great the victim's sufferings in the throes of it, the moment relief comes it is found to be no relief at all. I believe that the wondrous wise man in the nursery rhyme must have been suffering from *cacoëthes scribendi*. 'He jumped into a bramble bush and scratched out both his eyes,' was merely a pictorial way of saying that he found the disease intolerable and took heroic measures to effect a cure. Having regained his health, he found that condition even less tolerable and at once elected to become ill again.

I have heard it said that an infallible and permanent cure for the malady is the cooling salve of public indifference and neglect. Cooling this unguent undoubtedly is; but healing? I doubt it. One thinks of innumerable instances that lead to a contrary opinion: of men, some of them rich in worldly goods and therefore under no compulsion to write; others wretchedly poor; some with remarkable and varied gifts; some with a meager fraction of a talent, but all of them having this in common — that they spent their lives in obscure and solitary literary toil without once having heard a heartening shout of public acclaim.

Consider, for a moment, a particular and by no means an exceptional case, that of Samuel Butler. Although he sometimes wrote music or painted pictures, he was first and last a literary man, and during his life he published fourteen books, all at his own expense. 'Erewhon' alone netted him a small profit, and the return from that was only sixty-two pounds and some odd shillings. The others were total failures, commercially. Butler was out of pocket 779 pounds, 18 shillings, one-and-a-half pence for the lot of them. He kept a careful record of his expenditures and knew even to a ha'pence what his books had cost him. After 'Erewhon' his most successful book was 'Life and Habit,' which found 640 purchasers, and the least successful, a volume of essays of which not a single copy was sold. Nevertheless, Butler continued writing to the end of his days. There is an interesting note in his 'Journal' published after his death, with reference to his books and how they came to be written. 'I never make them,' he said; 'they grow; they come to me and insist upon being written, and on being such and such. I did not want to write "Erewhon." I wanted to go on painting and found it an abominable nuisance being dragged willy-nilly into writing it. So with all my books — the subjects were never of my own choosing; they pressed themselves upon me with more force than I could resist.'

Mr. Arthur Machen, author of those strange tales, 'The Great God Pan,' 'The Hill of Dreams,' 'The Secret Glory,' etc., furnishes another example of a man who was not deterred from writing by the lack of public encouragement. He resembles Samuel Butler in that his peculiar temperament and the outward circumstances of his life seem to have made it necessary that he should write the books he did write and only those. Although he is an artist in a small and lonely field, for lifelong devotion to the task of cultivating its grudging soil, I doubt whether his equal can be found in the history of letters.

Certainly, there has never been a more indomitable sufferer from the scourge, *cacoëthes scribendi*. His volume of reminiscences contains a passage that needs to be quoted, it puts so well the case for all men of limited talent who are searching for a way to the full heaven of Art which is never to be theirs:

> No; the only course is to go on stumbling and struggling and blundering like a man lost in a dense thicket on a dark night; a thicket, I say, of rebounding boughs that punish with the sting of a whip-lash, of thorns that savagely lacerate the flesh — it is the flesh of the heart, alas! that they tear — of sharp rocks of agony and black pools of despair. Such is the obscure wood of the literary life; such, at least, it was to me. You struggle to find your way; but again and again you ask yourself whether, for you, there is any way. You think you have hit upon the lucky track at last. And lo! before your feet is the black pit. And such is not alone the adventure of little, ineffectual, struggling men. How old was glorious Cervantes, now serene forever amongst the immortals, when he found his way to that village of La Mancha? Fifty, I think, or almost fifty. And he had been struggling for years to write plays, poetry, and short stories of passion and sentiment; and it was only the roar of applause that thundered up from the world when the Knight and the Squire were seen riding over the hill that convinced Cervantes that at last he had discovered his true path; if indeed he were ever convinced of the magnitude and majesty of the achievement of 'Don Quixote.'
>
> And if these things are done with the great, what will be done with the little? If the clear-voiced leaders of the everlasting choir are to suffer so and agonize, what of miserable little Welchmen stammering and stuttering by the Wandle, in the obscure rectory among the hills, in waste places by Shepherd's Bush, in gloomy Great Russell Street, where the ghosts of dead, disappointed authors go sighing to and fro? For the fate of the little literary man there is no articulate speech that is sufficient; one must fall back on aoi, or oimoi, or alas, or some such vague lament of unutterable woe.

It is a pity that no one competent to do so has made a thorough study, historically and pathologically, of the *cacoëthes scribendi*. If such a study is ever made, Mr. Machen's two volumes, 'Things Near and Far,' and 'Far-Off Things,' should be consulted. He goes into the facts of his own case with painstaking thoroughness, and has reached certain conclusions that need to be tested in the light of wider evidence. For example: like Samuel Butler he kept a careful record of his returns from the sale of his books. He runs through the list of these books, written between the years, 1880 and 1922, and finds that there are eighteen titles. His total receipts from these eighteen volumes, which cost him forty-two years of toil, amounted to the sum of 635 pounds. In other words, for nearly half a century of labour, he had been paid at the rate of fifteen pounds and a few shillings per annum. 'It seems clear,' he adds, 'that my literary activities cannot be adequately accounted for on the hypothesis of mere greed and money-grubbing.'

Then he wonders what the motive, or motives, can be that induce men to devote their lives to literature; why it is that so many writers are willing to endure poverty, disappointment, mortification and despair for such slender rewards, for no reward, in fact, that could be adequate. And his conclusion is this: that life, if looked at honestly, without flinching, is intolerable; and that men will do anything to hide from the serious facts of life, 'follow any track, however perilous or painful, if only these serious facts can be evaded or forgotten, though it be but for a few hours.' To write books is one method of escape — of hard escape, to be sure, but offering certain advantages to certain types of men.

I question the validity of this conclusion, not in particular instances, but as a general statement of the case. Life is not so horrible as this comes to. Rabelais, Cervantes, Charles Dickens, the three writers whom Mr. Machen loves and reveres above all others, relished life keenly, and their huge capacity for loving it is one of the measures of their greatness as artists. I do not believe that the writing of books was an attempt at escape on their part. I should think the purpose was, rather, to convince men of the folly of wishing to escape, by showing them the value of the gift of life, whether considered as stirring adventure or a fascinating spectacle. I doubt whether any sweeping statement can be made with respect to the causes of *cacoëthes scribendi*. They seem to be as many and as varied as the victims.

One of the most eminent of these victims, Joseph Conrad, would have been the last, surely, to have agreed with Mr. Machen that a literary career offers a means of escape from the keener sufferings of life. His letters, many of them written in the midst of his work, reveal a man often suffering, as an artist, the keenest torments. There were, to be sure, contributory causes: ill health, worry about money, and the like, but these by no means account for such anguish of mind and spirit. No one familiar with Conrad's work could have been unprepared for the revelations of the letters, but I doubt whether many of his readers had any conception of the grievous cost to him of the act of creation. He did, once, give us a glimpse behind the scenes. In his autobiographical narrative, 'A Personal Record,' speaking of the labour it cost him to write 'Nostromo,' he said:

> For twenty months, neglecting the common joys of life that fall to the lot of the humblest on this earth, I had, like the prophet of old, 'wrestled with the Lord' for my creation, for the headlands of the coast, for the darkness of the Placid Gulf, the light on the snows, the clouds in the sky, and for the breath of life that had to

be blown into the shapes of men and women, of Latin and Saxon, of Jew and Gentile. These are, perhaps, strong words, but it is difficult to characterize, otherwise, the intimacy and strain of a creative effort in which mind and will and conscience are engaged to the full, hour after hour, day after day, away from the world, and to the exclusion of all that makes life really lovable and gentle — something for which a material parallel can only be found in the everlasting sombre stress of the westward winter passage round Cape Horn.

It would be an excellent thing if this passage, suitably printed and framed, were to be hung on the walls of classrooms wherever English literature is studied and the art of writing professedly taught. It is reasonable to suppose that students, reading it and pondering it, day after day, would gain some conception of the difficulties of the tasks confronting a serious writer, of the nature of the gifts necessary to conquer them, and of the *peine forte et dure* which is his portion in life. If, as a result, some of them were to be deterred from undertaking literary careers, what a blessing that would be, both to themselves and to the reading public!

For there is no doubt that *cacoëthes scribendi* is becoming all too common a malady in our day. In most cases it is now, indeed, as the lexicographers define it: 'an itch for doing something inadvisable.' All of us journeymen scribblers are out of the discussion, of course. We are merely artisans, like blacksmiths, or carpenters, or bricklayers; but every year, larger and yet larger numbers of young men and women appear who wish and demand to be taken seriously; and the amazing thing is that they *are* taken seriously. So great are their numbers that the army of literary folk threatens eventually to include the whole of our adult and adolescent population. Most of them are wholly lacking in the gifts for their high calling, save, occasionally, in that of dogged persistence. The importance of this quality becomes exaggerated in their eyes. They believe it to be half the battle when, in reality, it is not one-quarter of it. And it is nothing at all, of course, without at least an additional quarter of ability.

I sometimes think that liberty to aspire, supposed to be among the crowning glories of our democratic era, is really among the most doubtful of its blessings. Certainly it is responsible for a great deal of needless misery. Consider this army of would-be artists so many of them trying to stretch meager gifts to the limit of their aspirations; or, worse, creating gifts for themselves out of pure imagination. If they were denied the opportunity how much happier they would be and how much disappointment would be spared them! There is a definition of Art to be found in one of Mr. Santayana's 'Dialogues in Limbo,' which, I think, should also be brought to the attention of young literary aspirants. It is this: 'Art, which is action guided by knowledge, is the principle of benefit, and without art, the freer a man is the more miserable he must become.' Action guided by knowledge, more particularly, by self-knowledge, is precisely the kind of art so many of us know nothing about, and that is why we lead such futile and inartistic lives — why, for example, we think ourselves sufferers from *cacoëthes scribendi* when our complaint is merely misguided and inordinate ambition, having not the least resemblance to this glorious disease.

The worst periods of the authentic complaint must be, surely, when feelings of despair and chilling doubt as to the value of his work, visit the sufferer. Then it must be a dread scourge indeed. The poets are least to be pitied at such times, for, usually, they need not suffer in silence, misery feeding on misery. They may find solace in pain-relieving song concerning the disease itself. English poetry is full of instances where this has been done; there come into mind at once those noble and moving lines from Francis Thompson's 'The Cloud's Swan Song':

> Like grey clouds one by one my songs upsoar
> Over my soul's cold peaks; and one by one
> They loose their little rain, and are no more;
> And whether well or ill, to tell me there is none.
>
> For 'tis an alien tongue, of alien things,
> From all men's care how miserably apart!
> Even my friends say: 'Of what is this he sings?'
> And barren is my song, and barren is my heart.
>
> For who can work, unwitting his work's worth?
> Better, meseems, to know the work for naught,
> Turn my sick course back to the kindly earth,
> And leave to ampler plumes the jetting tops of thought.

What a gulf lies between accomplishment and the ideal conception! What misgivings must assail the heart of every artist as he views his creations in the cold light of accomplished fact! Here, I think, we have the explanation why *cacoëthes scribendi* is a disease only to be cured by death. Every artist, however profound his despair, is spurred on again and again in efforts to realize his dreams. He will never succeed of course, but he will never accept defeat.

GEORGE MOORE

Books are like individuals; you know at once if they are going to create a sense within the sense, to fever, to madden you in blood and brain, or if they will merely leave you indifferent, or irritable, having unpleasantly disturbed sweet intimate musings as might a draught from an open window.

JOHN LIVINGSTON LOWES
extols the brave new world of books as an antidote to the restless and exigent mood of today.

OF READING BOOKS

THE text (if I may call it so) of what I mean to say is this: 'I hope, y-wis, to rede... som day.' Which, translated into the vernacular, means: 'I hope to Heaven that some day I'll get a chance to *read*.' That pious hope is part of a line of Chaucer, and unless I much mistake, it finds an ardent response in the minds of scores of us today, who find ourselves caught in the toils of a more restless and exigent century than his. And what I propose to say about reading — whether it be for delight, or for information, or for something deeper still — must, if it is to have any value, take into account conditions which all save a few happy mortals are destined to meet.

I

For we live in an age and a land above all things marked by hurried motion. I happened to come from Pittsburgh to New York the other day, at the rate of fifty miles an hour. Every few minutes another train flashed by in the opposite direction. On a hundred thousand miles of rails the same flying shuttles were hurtling back and forth. The taxi which took me from one station to another in New York was numbered (they know better now) one million seven hundred thousand and odd, and the other million or so were trying simultaneously to hurl themselves along the streets. And under the street, packed trains, a couple of minutes or so apart, were crashing back and forth in the din of steel on steel flung back from walls of stone. My neighbour in the smoking-car that morning was manfully ploughing his way through a Gargantuan Sunday paper. My eye caught a page-wide headline in one of those instructive sections which temper the comic supplement to the inquiring spirit: 'Power enough in a glass of water to drive an ocean liner.' And I wondered how far and how fast, when science had done its worst, our harmless necessary glass of water in the morning might one day drive us! A sip before breakfast here in Boston, and in an instant, if we will it, we are catapulted to Chicago. Why not? That is the logical goal of our endeavours. The word of the hour is the word of my headline — 'drive.' To carry on the business of college, church, or hospital, we initiate a 'drive.' Even in religion, education, and philanthropy we tend to think and act in terms of energy translated into tense and often fevered motion. The thing meets us everywhere. 'In a weekly paper not very long ago' — and now I am quoting William James — 'I remember reading a story in which, after describing the beauty and interest of the heroine's personality, the author summed up her charms by saying that to all who looked upon her an impression as of "bottled lightning" was irresistibly conveyed. Bottled lightning, in truth,' William James goes on, 'is one of our American ideals, even of a young girl's character!' That was twenty-five years ago. Today, be they masculine or feminine, we dub such persons dynamos. And the human dynamo is fast becoming our ideal.

Matthew Arnold saw all this coming — saw it, indeed, already well under way — much more than fifty years ago. 'O born in days when wits were fresh and clear,' he cries in his 'Scholar-Gipsy,'

> And life ran gaily as the sparkling Thames;
>   Before *this strange disease of modern life,*
> *With its sick hurry, its divided aims,*
>   *Its heads o'ertax'd, its palsied hearts,* was rife —
> Fly hence, our contact fear!...

And he continues

> But fly our paths, our feverish contact fly!
>   For strong is the infection of our mental strife.

And in these last lines Arnold puts his finger on the core of the malady, so far as we are concerned. For this tension in which today we live and move and have our being is contagious. And there Matthew Arnold is at one with William James, in that wise discourse on which I have already drawn — his talk to students on 'The Gospel of Relaxation': 'The American overtension and jerkiness and breathlessness and intensity,' he declares, 'are primarily social... phenomena. They are *bad habits*... bred of custom and example.' And you know, and I know, that high tension *is* contagious, and that we move in an atmosphere charged with energy driving at action, which sets us driving too, whether we are geared to anything or not. And we are helpless, unless — but that is to anticipate. And now I come back for a moment to Arnold again:

> But we, brought forth and rear'd in hours
>   Of change, alarm, surprise —
> What shelter to grow ripe is ours?
>   What leisure to grow wise?

> Like children bathing on the shore,
>   Buried a wave beneath,
> The second wave succeeds, before
>   We have had time to breathe.
>
> Too fast we live, too much are tried,
>   Too harass'd, to attain
> Wordsworth's sweet calm, or Goethe's wide
>   And luminous view to gain.

And that brings us within sight of our theme.

For one of the consequences of this modern malady of ours is that the gracious things which lend to life and human intercourse the beauty of serenity and comeliness are gone, or on the wane. 'The wisdom of a learned man,' wrote the author of Ecclesiasticus long centuries ago, 'cometh by opportunity of leisure,' and not wisdom only, but grace, and gentle breeding, and amenity, and poise come so, and only so. And leisure (which is not to be confused with empty time, but which is time through which free, life-enhancing currents flow) — leisure in these days is something to be sought and cherished as a rare and priceless boon; leisure to think, and talk, and write, and read — lost arts else, all of them. 'John Wesley's conversation is good,' said Doctor Johnson to Boswell once, 'but he is never at leisure. He is always obliged to go at a certain hour. This is very disagreeable to a man who loves to fold his legs and have out his talk, as I do.' The sainted John Wesley in the rôle of a modern 'hustler' is a little humorous, and Samuel Johnson did a certain amount of work himself. But an age that loved, on occasion, to fold its legs, and have its talk out, and its book out, and its delightful familiar letters out, may not have been one hundred per cent efficient (in our devastating modern phrase), but it did have shelter to grow ripe, and it did have leisure to grow wise, and more than our own driving, restless period, it did possess its soul. 'He hasteth well,' wrote Chaucer, whom business could not make dull, 'who wisely can abide,' and we first learn to live when we

>   ... claim not every laughing Hour
> For handmaid to [our] striding power...
> To usher for a destined space
> (*Her own sweet errands all forgone*)
> The too imperious traveller on.

'We are great fools,' says Montaigne: ' "He spends his life in idleness," we say, "I've *done* nothing today." What! Have you not *lived?* That is not only the most fundamental, but the most illustrious of your occupations.'

Our salvation, then, lies in the refusal to be forever hurried with the crowd, and in our resolution to step out of it at intervals, and drink from deeper wells. 'Il se faut reserver une arrière boutique, toute nostre, toute franche' — 'we ought to reserve for ourselves an *arrière boutique*, a back-shop, all our own, all free, in which we may set up our own true liberty and principal retreat and solitude.' That is Montaigne's ripe, leisured wisdom, and in that *arrière boutique* the wish: 'I hope, y-wis, to rede... som day,' may find accomplishment. And so I mean to talk for a little while, most informally and most unacademically, about reading — a subject which, partly through our fault, I fear, some of you have come to think of in terms of courses and degrees, but which is infinitely bigger than all that. It is not even scholarship that I shall have in mind. It is simply reading, as men and women have always read, for the delight of it, and for the consequent enriching and enhancement of one's life. I have put delight deliberately first, for the rest, I believe, is contingent upon that. 'In general,' said Goethe once, 'we learn from what we love.' And I propose first of all to exhibit some lovable readers — not a Professor or even a Doctor in the lot, I think — and allow them to speak for themselves. And first, then, reading for the sheer delight of it.

II

'In anything fit to be called by the name of reading,' says Stevenson in his delectable 'Gossip on Romance,'

> the process itself should be absorbing and voluptuous; we should gloat over a book, be rapt clean out of ourselves, and rise from the perusal, our mind filled with the busiest, kaleidoscopic dance of images, incapable of sleep or of continuous thought. It was for this... that we read so closely, and loved our books so dearly, in the bright, troubled period of boyhood.... We dug blithely after a certain sort of incident, like a pig for truffles. For my part, I liked a story to begin with an old wayside inn where, toward the close of the 'year 17—,' several gentlemen in three-cocked hats were playing bowls. A friend of mine preferred the Malabar coast in a storm, with a ship beating to windward, and a scowling fellow of Herculean proportions striding along the beach —

and so on delightfully. Now it is that unquenchable, bubbling zest on which I wish for the moment to insist, and Stevenson's is the gusto of 'the bright, troubled period of boyhood.' Let us set beside it, as is fitting, its companion piece. 'But, my dearest Catherine' — and need I say that it is the immortal and adorable Jane Austen who is speaking —

> 'But, my dearest Catherine, what have you been doing with yourself all this morning? Have you gone on with "Udolpho"?'
> 'Yes, I have been reading it ever since I woke; and I am got to the black veil.'

'Are you indeed? How delightful! Oh, I would not tell you what is behind the black veil for the world! Are you not wild to know?'

'Oh! yes, quite; what can it be? But do not tell me. I would not be told upon any account. I know it must be a skeleton; I am sure it is Laurentina's skeleton. Oh, I am delighted with the book! I should like to spend my whole life in reading it, I assure you; if it had not been to meet you, I would not have come away from it for all the world.'

'Dear creature, how much I am obliged to you! and when you have finished "Udolpho," we will read "The Italian" together; and I have made out a list of ten or twelve more of the same kind for you.'

'Have you indeed? How glad I am! What are they all?'

'I will read you their names directly. Here they are, in my pocket-book: "Castle of Wolfenbach," "Clermont," "Mysterious Warnings," "Necromancer of the Black Forest," "Midnight Bell," "Orphan of the Rhine," and "Horrid Mysteries." Those will last us some time.'

'Yes, pretty well; but are they all horrid? Are you sure they are all horrid?'

'Yes, quite sure; for a particular friend of mine, a Miss Andrews, a sweet girl, one of the sweetest creatures in the world, has read every one of them.'

Well, that is the meat upon which your inveterate readers are apt to have fed in childhood, and happy are you, if you have been caught at it young. For romances, and stories of giants, magicians, and genii, read with a child's quick and plastic imagination, are stepping-stones to later, deeper, if no more enduring loves. 'I read through all gilt-cover little books that could be had at that time,' wrote Coleridge to Tom Poole in those precious fragments of an autobiography,

> and likewise all the uncovered tales of Tom Hickathrift, Jack the Giant Killer, and the like. And I used to lie by the wall, and

mope; and my spirits used to come upon me suddenly and in a flood — and then I was accustomed to run up and down the churchyard, and act over again all I had been reading on the docks, the nettles, and the rank grass. At six years of age... I found the Arabian Nights' Entertainments... and I distinctly recollect the anxious and fearful eagerness with which I used to watch the window where the book lay, and when the sun came upon it, I would seize it, carry it by the wall, and bask, and read. ... My whole being was, with eyes closed to every object of present sense, to crumple myself up in a sunny corner, and read, read, read.

I know there are those to whom all this is heresy, and who would feed children pedagogically desiccated food. There have always been such earnest and misguided souls. Charles Lamb has a gloriously volcanic outburst, in a letter to Coleridge, about Mrs. Barbauld's edifying books for children — Mrs. Barbauld, who objected to 'The Ancient Mariner' because it was improbable, and who rushed in where angels fear to tread with 'An Address to the Deity':

I am glad [he writes] the snuff and Pi-pos's books please. 'Goody Two Shoes' is almost out of print. Mrs. Barbauld's stuff has banished all the old classics of the nursery.... Knowledge insignificant and vapid as Mrs. B's books convey, it seems, must come to a child in the *shape* of *knowledge*, and his empty noddle must be turned with conceit of his own powers when he has learnt that a Horse is an animal, and Billy is better than a Horse, and such like: instead of that beautiful Interest in wild tales which made the child a man, while all the time he suspected himself to be no bigger than a child. Science has succeeded to Poetry no less in the little walks of children than with men. Is there no possibility of averting this sore evil? Think what you would have been now, if instead of being fed with Tales and old wives' fables in childhood, you had been crammed with geography and natural history!

Damn them! [The Bowdlerizing editors print 'Hang them' — but Lamb was righteously indignant, and did *not* write 'Hang'] — I mean the cursed Barbauld Crew, those Blights and Blasts of all that is Human in man and child.

That at least cannot be charged with ambiguity, but Lamb expressed himself again — this time with reference to a girl's reading:

> She was tumbled early [he is writing of Bridget Elia, who was Mary Lamb], by accident or design, into a spacious closet of good old English reading, without much selection or prohibition, and browsed at will upon that fair and wholesome pasturage. Had I twenty girls, they should be brought up exactly in this fashion. I know not whether their chance in wedlock might not be diminished by it; but I can answer for it that it makes (if the worst come to the worst) most incomparable old maids.

On that point I venture no opinion, but the doctrine of the rest is sound.

Now I have dwelt on this seemingly irrelevant theme of early reading, because the element of delight is the point I wish just now to emphasize, and that eager, childlike zest, once caught, is seldom lost. There is no essential difference, for example, between Coleridge's absorption in the 'Arabian Nights,' and the irrepressible gusto with which John Keats read Shakespeare. Here is a bit of a letter which Keats wrote from Burford Bridge, one moonlit night, while he was deep in the composition of 'Endymion':

> One of the three books I have with me is Shakespeare's Poems: I never found so many beauties in the Sonnets — they seem to be full of fine things said unintentionally — in the intensity of working out conceits. Is this to be borne? Hark ye!

> When lofty trees I see barren of leaves,
> Which erst from heat did canopy the head,
> And Summer's green all girded up in sheaves,
> Borne on the bier with white and bristly head.

He has left nothing to say about nothing or anything: for look at snails — you know what he says about Snails — you know when he talks about 'cockled Snails' — well, in one of these sonnets, he says — the chap slips into — no! I lie! this is in the 'Venus and Adonis': the simile brought it to my Mind.

> As the snail, whose tender horns being hit,
> Shrinks back into his shelly cave with pain....

He overwhelms a genuine Lover of poesy with all manner of abuse, talking about —

> 'a poet's rage
> And stretched metre of an antique song.'

Which, by the bye, will be a capital motto for my poem, won't it?... By the Whim-King! I'll give you a stanza —

and at once he is off creating! That is Keats through and through — the Keats who went 'ramping' (as Cowden Clarke put it) through the 'Faerie Queene'; who 'hoisted himself up, and looked burly and dominant, as he said, "What an image that is - *sea-shouldering whales*"'; who wrote, the night he first opened Chapman's Homer: 'Then felt I like some watcher of the skies When a new planet swims into his ken.' I always think, when I read in Keats's letters the things he says about his books, of those lines in 'Ruth':

> Before me shone a glorious world —
> Fresh as a banner bright, unfurled
> To music suddenly.

I have known, *you* know, men and women — busy men and women, too — to whom a book still means that. It is the very spirit of Miranda's cry:

> O wonder!
> How many goodly creatures are there here!
> How beauteous mankind is! O brave new world,
> That has such people in't!

And I envy any one to whom for the first time — or for the hundredth time — the brave new world of books is opening, that world which has such people in it: Cleopatra, Mr. Pickwick, Helen of Troy, Samuel Pepys, the Wife of Bath, Sir John Falstaff, Mrs. Proudie, Sir Willoughby Patterne, Becky Sharp, Perdita, Pantagruel, Mephistopheles, Launcelot, Dido, and a thousand others more alive than you and I. 'I doe nothing without blithenesse,' wrote Montaigne in his essay on 'Books' — and if I were going to that famous desert island for which we are periodically asked to select our five-foot shelf, Montaigne in his pithy, sinewy, succulent French would be almost the first whom I should pick — 'Je ne fay rien sans gayeté'; and no mortal ever went adventuring more blithely among books than Michael Montaigne, or brought home richer treasure-trove.

'But,' you will say to me, 'we haven't time.' I know it; very few of us these days have time — those least, I sometimes think, who have it most. But even if, being modern, and ambitious, and efficient, and all that, we are whirled along with our fellow atoms in the rush, we shall not be losing time if now and then we pause, and loaf (I wish the fine phrase had not been worn so trite), loaf, and invite our souls. And if you worship in the temple of efficiency, don't forget — and again I am drawing on the wise humanity of William James — that 'just as a bicycle chain may be too tight, so may one's carefulness and conscientiousness be so tense as to hinder the running of one's mind.' And after all, the smooth, free running of one's mind is fairly important to the precious efficiency of whatever machinery it be that your particular intelligence helps to run. Even as a business proposition (to fall again into the jargon of the day), time spent in unclamping our mental processes is time won, and not time lost.

And the thing is possible. Here is part of a letter which Matthew Arnold wrote to his sister. And Arnold, being a hard-driven public official, knew whereof he spoke.

> If I were you, my dear Fan, I should now take to some regular reading, if it were only an hour a day. It is the best thing in the world to have something of this sort as a point in the day, and far too few people know and use this secret. You would have your district still, and all your business as usual, but you would have this hour in your day in the midst of it all, and it would soon become of the greatest solace to you.

There is none of us for whom, with occasional lapses, that is not possible. And the last thing on earth that I am suggesting is that this hour be made a task — something to which we bind ourselves, with grim conscientiousness, as to one relentless duty more. I am not forgetting that I am still speaking of reading for the sheer delight of it, and to come down to cases is worth considerably more than further homiletics. This, from a letter of Edward Fitzgerald, is the sort of thing I mean:

> Here is a glorious sunshiny day: all the morning I read about Nero in Tacitus, lying at full length on a bench in the garden: a nightingale singing, and some red anemones eyeing the sun manfully not far off. A funny mixture all this: Nero and the delicacy of spring: all very human however.

Well, it *is* human, and the sort of reading which just now I have in mind is a creature not too bright and good even for human nature's daily food. Here is a passage in which William Hazlitt is talking of luxuriating in books:

> I remember sitting up half the night to read 'Paul and Virginia,' which I picked up at an inn at Bridgewater, after being drenched in the rain all day; and at the same place I got through two volumes of Madame D'Arblay's 'Camilla.' It was on the 10th of April, 1798, that I sat down to a volume of the 'New Eloise,' at the inn at Llangollen, over a bottle of sherry and a cold chicken.

And that delectable epicureanism is one of the marks of your true reader for delight — he remains a human being while he reads. There is Browning:

> Then I went in-doors, brought out a loaf,
> Half a cheese, and a bottle of Chablis;
> Lay on the grass and forgot the oaf
> Over a jolly chapter of Rabelais.

And here is Charles Lamb to Coleridge:

> Observe, there comes to you, by the Kendal waggon to-morrow ... a box, containing the Miltons, the strange American Bible... Baxter's 'Holy Commonwealth,' for which you stand indebted to me 3s. 6d.; an odd volume of Montaigne, being of no use to me, I having the whole; certain books belonging to Wordsworth, as do also the strange thick-hoofed shoes, which are very much admired at in London —

and there I must pause for a moment. For those thick-hoofed shoes are uncanny in their rich suggestiveness. They are Simon Lee and Goody Blake and the Idiot Boy and Peter Bell in a nutshell. And one of the fascinations of the letters — of Gray's inimitable raciness, of 'the divine chit-chat of Cowper,' as Coleridge calls it, of Lamb, Byron, Keats, Fitzgerald, Stevenson — one of the quintessential pleasures of the letters lies in their wealth of unexpected flashes: 'fine things said unintentionally,' as Keats said of the Sonnets. And now I return to Lamb and his box of books:

> If you find the Miltons in certain parts dirtied and soiled with a crumb of right Gloucester blacked in the candle (my usual supper), or peradventure a stray ash of tobacco wafted into the crevices, look to that passage more especially: depend upon it, it contains good matter.

Crumbs of toasted cheese and the ash of a pipe suggest, however, concomitant delights perhaps of scant appeal to certain readers. Well, then, here is Dorothy Wordsworth:

> Worked hard, and read 'Midsummer Night's Dream,' and ballads. Sauntered a little in the garden. The blackbird sate quietly in its nest, rocked by the wind, and beaten by the rain.... Sauntered a good deal in the garden, bound carpets, mended old clothes, read 'Timon of Athens,' dried linen.... In the afternoon we sate by the fire; I read Chaucer aloud, and Mary read the first canto of the 'Faerie Queene.'... We spent the morning in the orchard reading the 'Epithalamium' of Spenser; walked backwards and forwards.... We sowed the scarlet beans in the orchard, and read 'Henry V' there. After dinner William added one to the orchard steps.... A sunshiny morning. I walked to the top of the hill and sate under a wall ... facing the sun. I read a scene or two in 'As You Like It.'... Read part of 'The Knight's Tale' with exquisite delight.

'The Faerie Queene,' the 'Epithalamium,' 'Henry V,' 'As You Like It,' 'The Knight's Tale': those are the things that you 'take,' as if they were some academic whooping-cough or measles. And here, under no compulsion, is a woman reading them as if they'd actually been written to be *read* — reading them by the fire, in the orchard, on a hill-top under a wall in the sun — reading with exquisite delight. Heaven help us who teach, if through well-meant but sometimes misguided efforts to instruct, we have rubbed the bloom off the great books, and blunted the keen edge of pleasure such as that!

I have not the slightest intention in all this of implying that only the hundred best books, so to speak, will serve our purposes. Some of the most bewitching, completely captivating things in life lie buried in forgotten, relatively worthless books, if one has eyes to see them. An enterprising young friend of mine suggested in a letter that I had from him not long ago the alluring enterprise of an anthology of the *worst* poetry. I hope he will make it! For your true adventurer in 'the wide, wild wilderness of books' knows that often, as Browning has it, 'the worst turns the best for the brave.' 'I am going to repeat my old experiment,' Stevenson wrote in a letter to Sidney Colvin, 'after buckling to a while to write more correctly, lie down and have a wallow.' That is not elegant, but it is precise. And after one has wound up one's faculties, like Mrs. Battle, over serious things, one may indulge with propriety in what I suppose one may designate as a slumming expedition among books. I do not recommend it as a practice, but for occasional indulgence there are distinguished precedents. Macaulay, for instance, besides knowing the romances of a certain prolific Mrs. Meeke almost by heart, was devoted to the literary efforts of a Mrs. Kitty Cuthbertson — 'Santo Sebastiano, or, the Young Protector,' 'The Forest of Montalbano,' 'The Romance of the Pyrenees,' 'Adelaide, or, the Countercharm.' And on the last page of his edition of 'Santo Sebastiano' appears an elaborate computation of the number of fainting fits that occur in the course of the five volumes. Here they are:

Julia de Clifford	11
Lady Delamore	4
Lady Theodosia	4
Lord Glenbrook	2
Lord Delamore	2
Lady Enderfield	1
Lord Ashgrove	1
Lord St. Orville	1
Henry Mildmay	1 —

a total of 27. And here is a specimen of one of these catastrophes: 'One of the sweetest smiles that ever animated the face of mortal now diffused itself over the countenance of Lord St. Orville, as he fell at the feet of Julia in a deathlike swoon.'

There is a volume entitled 'A Spiritual Diary and Soliloquies' by a certain John Ruttey, M.D., which, Boswell informs us, diverted Doctor Johnson vastly — one of these priceless things on which one stumbles now and then, and which reward excursions off the beaten path. Here are a few of the worthy Quaker's entries:

Tenth month, 1753.
23. Indulgence in bed an hour too long.
Twelfth month, 17. An hypochondriac obnubilation from wind and indigestion.
Ninth month, 28. An over-dose of whiskey.
29. [Which was the day after the over-dose] A dull, cross, choleric day.
First month, 22. A little swinish at dinner and repast.
31. Dogged on provocation.
Second month, 5. Very dogged or snappish...
23. Dogged again.
Fourth month, 29. Mechanically and sinfully dogged.

And here is an unillustrious sheaf of my own, gleaned from one of the most absurd, yet seductive volumes ever penned, Henry

Mackenzie's 'Man of Feeling.' The following sentences fall within two paragraphs: 'Though this story was told in very plain language, it had particularly attracted Harley's notice; he had given it the tribute of some tears.' In the same paragraph an unfortunate Ophelia-like lady sings: 'There was a plaintive wildness in the air not to be withstood; and, except the keeper's, there was not an unmoistened eye around her.' After three more sentences: 'She stretched out her hand to Harley; he pressed it between both of his, and bathed it with his tears.' In the same paragraph. 'Harley looked on his ring. He put a couple of guineas into the man's hand: "Be kind to that unfortunate." He burst into tears and left them.' A few pages later on: 'He laid his left hand on his heart — the sword dropped from his right — he burst into tears.' In the next paragraph: 'The desperation that supported her was lost; she fell to the ground, and bathed his feet with her tears.' In the following paragraph: 'Nature at last prevailed, he fell on her neck, and mingled his tears with hers.' On the next page: 'As he spoke these last words, his voice trembled in his throat; it was now lost in his tears.' A little later: 'The girl cried afresh; Harley kissed off her tears as they flowed, and wept between every kiss.' Finally: 'The old man now paused a moment to take breath. He eyed Harley's face; it was bathed with tears; the story was grown familiar to himself; *he dropped one tear, and no more.*' The exquisite economy of that solitary tear beggars admiration.

I am not, as you see, submitting a bibliography, or suggesting learned apparatus. For the moment we are concerned with reading for the sheer delight of it, when the world is all before us where to choose. But with delight there may be coupled something else. For one also reads to learn. And about that and one thing more, I shall be very brief.

III

Let me begin with a remark of Oliver Wendell Holmes:

> There are about as many twins in the births of thought as of children. For the first time in your lives you learn some fact or come across some idea. Within an hour, a day, a week, that same fact or idea strikes you from another quarter.... Yet no possible connection exists between the two channels by which the thought or the fact arrived.... And so it has happened to me and to every person, often and often, to be hit in rapid succession by these twinned facts or thoughts, as if they were linked like chain-shot.

Now all of us have had that experience, and it is apt to give us a curious sensation. 'Here,' we say, 'we've gone all our life without seeing that, and now all at once we see it at every turn. What does it mean?' Not long ago, for example, my attention was called for the first time, in a letter, to an international society of writers; two days later my eye caught a reference to it in a daily paper. Soon afterward I heard, for the first time to my knowledge, the name of a certain breed of terriers. Within a week I had come across the name in two different novels I was reading. What had happened? Simply this. I had doubtless seen both names time and again before, but nothing had ever stamped them on my memory, and so when they turned up again, they wakened no response. Then, all at once, something did fix them in my mind, and when they met my eye once more, they were there behind it, so to speak, to recognize themselves when they appeared. There had been set up in my brain, as it were, by each of them, a magnetic centre, ready to catch and attract its like.

Now one of the things which the process we call education ought to do, and by no means always does, is to establish in the mind as many as possible of these magnetic centres — live spots, which thrust out tentacles of association, and catch and draw to themselves their kind. For there are few joys in reading like the joy of the chase. And the joy of the chase comes largely through the action of these centres of association in your brain. Let me illustrate what I mean, and since first-hand experience imparts a certain vividness which abstract theorizing lacks, let me use myself as a *corpus vile*, and draw for a moment upon that.

Years ago, like everybody who was interested in Chaucer, I was puzzled by a mysterious reference to 'the dry sea and the Carrenar.' There was no Carrenar that anybody knew — nor, for that matter, any assured dry sea. One day, as I was reading in an old battered volume of 'Purchas his Pilgrimes' which is one of my choicest treasures, I was struck by the recurrence in a number of Central-Asian place-names, of the prefix 'Kara.' But none of them had the termination *nar*. Might they offer, however, a possible clue? So I asked that one among my colleagues who is an adept in all outlandish tongues, what the combination Kara-nar would mean in any language which he knew. The instant answer was: Black Lake. The rest of the long tale I shall not tell. Suffice it to say that there was and is a lake called Kara-nor; that it lay and lies off the great ancient trade-route between Orient and Occident, travelled in Chaucer's time; and that the lake is on the edge of a vast and terrible desert which was and is, in name and character, a veritable dry sea. And the sole reason of my mention of the business here is this: Had the crux of the Carrenar not been very much alive in my head, I might have seen a thousand Kara's in the travel-books without a thrill, and so have missed the most fascinating exploration — barring two — I ever undertook. And these other two came about in precisely the same way: through the recognition as I read of something which suggested, through a likeness recognized, the solution of a puzzle which had found a lodgment in my mind, and which was there, once more, to recognize its like, when, without warning, its like turned up. I cannot lay too strong an emphasis upon the sort of pleasure which results from the constant recognition in what one reads of things which link themselves, often in endlessly suggestive fashion, with things one has already read, till old friends with new faces meet us at every turn, and flash sudden light, and waken old associations, and quicken the zest for fresh adventures. To read with alert intellectual curiosity is one of the keenest joys of life, and it is pleasure which too many of us needlessly forgo.

Moreover, the dullest reading — and the world is full of very, very dull books, our share of which we are doomed to read as we are destined to meet our quota of bores in flesh and blood — the dullest books may become potential Ophirs and Golcondas, if we are looking for something as we read. If you know, every time you turn a page, that the thing you are looking for may leap to meet you on the next dull page, the task becomes an enthralling quest. There are few things more deadly in the world than the vast bulk of fourteenth-century French courtly verse. To read it just to read it — as we are in the habit of reading books — would bore the blithest spirit to extinction. Yet (to be personal again for the sake of first-hand testimony) I have read interminable masses of it again and again, each time with the sense of an adventure waiting beyond the next turn of the road, because each time I was on the trail of game — some clue, some corroboration of a guess, some evidence for this or that, which I hoped that I might find. Sometimes I have found it, sometimes not; but in any case the pages had the charm of a desert island in which at any moment one might stumble upon signs of buried gold. I remember one rapid reading of numerous volumes in search of examples of a certain phrase which had uncommonly engaging implications. I found them — but that was only half the game. For on almost every page all sorts of other things kept starting up, which fitted in with this, or which illuminated that — some of them of far more intrinsic value than the elusive trifle which I was tracking; and so the fly-leaves of my books were steadily filling, as I read, with references to still more fruitful possibilities for further explorations. And that leads me to say two things.

In the first place, one cannot begin too soon to buy one's own books, if for no other reason (and there are many more) than the freedom which they give you to use their fly-leaves for your own private index of those matters in their pages which are particularly yours, whether for interest, or information, or what not — those things which the index-makers never by any possibility include. To be able to turn at will, in a book of your own, to those passages which count for *you*, is to have your wealth at instant command, and your books become a record of your intellectual adventures, and a source of endless pleasure when you want, as you will, to turn back to the things which have given delight, or stirred imagination, or opened windows, in the past.

That is one point. The other is this. Goethe observed to Eckermann one day, in those 'Conversations' which constitute one of the most thought-provoking volumes in the world: 'You know, Saul the son of Kish went out one day to find his father's asses, and found a kingdom.' Which is a parable. For it is when you are looking for one thing as you read — it may be some utterly trivial affair — that ten to one you come upon the unexpected thing, the big or thrilling thing, which opens up new worlds of possibilities. Most of our discoveries — even if, as usually happens, they are discoveries only to us — are made when we are hot on the trail of something else. For because we are looking, we see, and we see more than we look for, because the eye which scans the page is actively alert to everything. And the more you *have* — the more live cluster-points of association there are in your brain — the more you see, and reading becomes a *cumulative* delight. 'The dear good people,' said Goethe once, 'don't know how long it takes to learn to read. I've been at it eighty years, and can't say yet that I've reached the goal.' One never does. There are always, as one goes on reading, unpath'd waters, undream'd shores ahead. And that is the secret of its perennial delight.

IV

One reads for the sheer enjoyment of it; one reads to learn; and there is a yet more excellent way. 'Man *lernt* nichts,' said Goethe of Winkelmann, 'wenn man ihn liest, aber man *wird* etwas' — 'you don't *learn* anything when you read him, but you *become* something.' That strikes to the very root of things, for it puts into one pregnant phrase the supreme creative influence in the world — the contagious touch of great personalities. And if a good book is, in truth, as Milton in a noble passage once declared, 'the precious life-blood of a master-spirit, embalmed and treasured up on purpose to a life beyond life,' then that creative influence of life on life is in the book, and as we read, our spirit is enriched and grows, and we *become* something. We are just a little ashamed these days, I know, in our reaction from a certain sort of cant, to read for our soul's sake, or our spirit's sake, or for edification, in the fine old sense of a sadly misused word. We feel, somehow, that it isn't quite the thing. Well, I don't care at all what terms you use; but we are more than intellect, and more than sense, and the deepest-lying springs of life are touched by life alone. And the men who have lived, and learned through living, and won through life a wide and luminous view — these men have the imperishable creative power of broadening, deepening, and enhancing life. They are the true humanists, and humanism, as I take it, is the development, not of scholars, not of philosophers, or scientists, or specialists in this or that, but of human beings. Goethe was such a humanist, and Goethe, by practice, not by precept, has pointed out the way.

'I read every year,' he said, 'a few plays of Molière, just as I also, from time to time, look over the engravings of the great Italian masters. For we little men aren't capable of maintaining within us the greatness of such things, and we have always to keep turning back to them from time to time, in order to quicken within us our impressions.' 'Today after dinner,' wrote Eckermann — and this sort of thing happened again and again — 'Goethe went through the portfolio of Raphael with me. He busies himself with Raphael very often, in order to keep himself always in touch with the best, and to exercise himself continually in thinking the thoughts of a great spirit after him.' And this, mind you, was not a preacher, or a teacher, or a reformer, but the most puissant, richly endowed spirit of the modern world. Beyond delight, and beyond intellectual adventure, there is the spiritual contagion of great books.

And again I should like to be very practical, for we live in a busy world. Matthew Arnold once wrote in a letter, while he was off inspecting schools: 'I enjoy my time here very much. I read five pages of Greek anthology every day, looking out all the words I do not know' — a very comforting remark, that last, for some of us. 'This,' he goes on, 'is what I shall always understand by *education*, and it does me good, and gives me great pleasure.' And the secret of his practice comes out in another letter, written this time to a British working man: 'As to useful knowledge, a single line of poetry, working in the mind, may produce more thought and lead to more light, which is what man wants, than the fullest acquaintance (to take your own instance) with the processes of digestion.' I am not sure, indeed, that anything which Arnold left is of more worth than his little, narrow, vest-pocket notebooks, which extend over a period of thirty-seven years. They served, not only for his record of engagements, but also as a repository for those passages of his daily reading which, in his own words, were 'working in his mind' — those passages through pondering on which (to use Montaigne's phrase) he *forged*, instead of merely *furnishing*, his soul. The entries for a dozen years have been printed, in a precious volume, by his daughter, and they exemplify, as nothing else I know can do, the sort of reading which I now have in mind — that reading through which 'man *wird* etwas.' I take nothing back of what I have said of reading as a delightful intellectual adventure. But this is different — yet not so different after all. 'I had an idea,' wrote Keats in one of his letters,

> that a Man might pass a very pleasant life in this manner — let him on a certain day read a certain Page of full Poesy or distilled Prose, and let him wander with it, and muse upon it, and reflect upon it, and bring home to it, and prophesy upon it, and dream upon it, until it becomes stale — but when will it do so? Never. When Man has arrived at a certain ripeness in intellect, any one

grand and spiritual passage serves him as a starting-point towards all 'the two-and-thirty Palaces.'

Well, there before you are the palaces and the road thereto. I don't know where, for you, they are; I only know they are there.

We have no shrines, most of us, any more — we Protestant-Puritan-Pagan-Anglo-Saxon Occidentals — no tranquil Buddhas or symbols of the passion by the roadside, no solemn temples, few cool, silent churches, always open and inviting to withdrawal for a moment from the hurly-burly of the world. It is not my business to determine whether that means loss or gain. But one thing it is always in our power to do — to withdraw now and then from the periphery to the centre, from the ceaseless whirl of the life that streams and eddies round us to the deep serenity of those great souls of better centuries ('ces grandes âmes des meilleurs siècles'), who give — and the lines sum up the antidote to the sick hurry of today — who give

> Authentic tidings of invisible things;
> Of ebb and flow, and ever-during power;
> And central peace, subsisting at the heart
> Of endless agitation.

WALT WHITMAN

The art of art, the glory of expression, and the sunshine of the light of letters is simplicity.

GEORGE GISSING

I know men who say they had as lief read any book in a library copy as in one from their own shelf. To me this is unintelligible.

ARCHIBALD MARSHALL

It is not a novelist's business to draw portraits but to present living figures, and the nearer he gets to the first the farther off he will be from the second.

JULIA NEWBURY

Never describe a person in detail; mention a few salient features and leave the rest to the imagination.

E. M. DELAFIELD

A novel is almost always invoked in my mind by one particular character.

HENDRIK WILLEM VAN LOON

I have never yet seen a book that I really wanted to read and which I didn't read.

LIST OF PUBLICATIONS

BOOKS BY HERBERT AGAR

1928   Milton and Plato.
        Fire and Sleet and Candlelight. (With Eleanor Carroll Chilton and Willis Fisher.)
1929   The Garment of Praise. (With Eleanor Carroll Chilton.)
1930   Bread and Circuses.
1933   The People's Choice.
1935   Land of the Free.

BOOKS BY GERTRUDE ATHERTON

1892   The Doomswoman.
1895   A Whirl Asunder.
1897   Patience Sparhawk and Her Times.
        His Fortunate Grace.
1898   The Californians.
        Transplanted.
1899   A Daughter of the Vine.
        The Valiant Runaways.
1900   Senator North.
1901   The Aristocrats.
1902   The Conqueror. (*Reissued* 1918.)
        The Splendid Idle Forties.
1903   A Few of Hamilton's Letters.
1904   Rulers of Kings.
1905   The Bell in the Fog.
        The Traveling Thirds.
1906   Rezanov. (*Reissued* 1934.)
1907   Ancestors.
1908   The Gorgeous Isle.
1910   Tower of Ivory.

1912 Julia France and Her Times.
1914 Perch of the Devil.
     California — An Intimate History.
1915 Before the Gringo Came.
1916 Mrs. Balfame.
1917 The Living Present.
1918 The White Morning.
1919 The Avalanche.
1921 Sisters in Law.
1922 Sleeping Fires.
1923 Black Oxen.
1925 The Crystal Cup.
1927 The Immortal Marriage.
1928 The Jealous Gods.
1929 Dido.
1931 The Sophisticates.
1932 Adventures of a Novelist. (*Reissued* 1935.)
1934 The Foghorn, and Other Stories.

BOOKS BY MARGARET AYER BARNES

1929 Prevailing Winds. (*Reissued* 1932.)
1930 Years of Grace.
1931 Westward Passage.
1933 Within This Present.
1935 Edna His Wife.

BOOKS BY PHYLLIS BOTTOME

1914 Broken Music.
     The Captive.
1916 The Dark Tower.
1917 The Derelict and Other Stories.
     The Second Fiddle.
1918 Helen of Troy and Rose.
1919 The Servant of Reality.

1921	The Crystal Heart.
1922	The Kingfisher.
1924	The Perfect Wife.
1925	Old Wine.
	Depth of Prosperity.
1927	The Belated Reckoning.
	The Rat.
	The Messenger of the Gods.
1928	Strange Fruit.
1929	Windlestraws.
1930	Tatter'd Loving.
1931	Devil's Due.
1933	The Advances of Harriet.
1934	Private Worlds.
	Innocence and Experience.

BOOKS BY JEANETTE EATON

1927	The Story of Transportation.
1928	The Story of Light.
1929	Daughter of the Seine; Life of Madame Roland
1931	The Warrior Saint; Life of Jeanne d'Arc.
	The Flame: Life of Saint Catherine of Siena.
1932	The Herdboy of Hungary. (With Alexander Finta.)
1933	Young Lafayette.
1934	Roland the Warrier. (With Virginia MacMakin Collier.)
1935	Behind the Show Window.

BOOKS BY HAVELOCK ELLIS

(Published by Houghton Mifflin Company)

1908	The Soul of Spain. (*Reissued* 1926, 1931.)
1911	The World of Dreams. (*Reissued* 1926.)
1912	The Task of Social Hygiene. (*Reissued* 1927.)
1914	Impressions and Comments. (*Reissued* 1926.)
1917	Affirmations. (*Reissued* 1926.)

1917 Essays in War Time.
1919 The Philosophy of Conflict.
1921 Impressions and Comments, Second Series. (*Reissued* 1926.)
1923 The Dance of Life. (*Reissued* 1925, 1926, 1929.)
1924 Impressions and Comments, Third Series. (*Reissued* 1929.)
1926 A Study of British Genius.
     The New Spirit.
1929 The Art of Life.
     Man and Woman.
1930 Fountain of Life.
1932 Views and Reviews.
1934 My Confessional.
1935 From Rousseau to Proust.

BOOKS BY ESTHER FORBES

1926 O Genteel Lady!
1928 A Mirror for Witches.
1935 Miss Marvel.

BOOKS BY FRANCES FROST

1929 Hemlock Wall.
1931 Blue Harvest.
1932 These Acres.
1933 Pool in the Meadow.
1934 Woman of This Earth.

BOOKS BY ELLEN GLASGOW

1897 The Descendant.
1898 Phases of an Inferior Planet.
1900 The Voice of the People.
1902 The Freeman and Other Poems.
     The Battle-Ground.
1904 The Deliverance.

1906	The Wheel of Life.
1908	Ancient Law.
1909	The Romance of a Plain Man.
1911	The Miller of Old Church.
1913	Virginia.
1916	Life and Gabriella.
1919	The Builders.
1922	One Man in His Time.
1923	The Shadowy Third.
1925	Barren Ground.
1926	The Romantic Comedians
1929	They Stooped to Folly.
1932	The Sheltered Life.
1935	Vein of Iron.

BOOKS BY JAMES NORMAN HALL

1916	Kitchener's Mob.
1918	High Adventure. (*Reissued* 1929.)
1920	The Lafayette Flying Corps. (With Charles B. Nordhoff.)
1926	On the Stream of Travel.
1928	Mid-Pacific.
1929	Falcons of France. (With Charles B. Nordhoff.)
1930	Flying with Chaucer.
	Mother Goose Land.
1932	Mutiny on the Bounty. (With Charles B. Nordhoff.)
1934	Men Against the Sea. (With Charles B. Nordhoff.)
	Pitcairn's Island. (With Charles B. Nordhoff.)
	The Tale of a Shipwreck.

BOOKS BY MARY AGNES HAMILTON

1912	Less Than the Dust.
	Greek Legends.
	The Story of Abraham Lincoln.
1913	Outlines of Greek and Roman History.

1914 Yes.
1917 Dead Yesterday.
1919 Full Circle.
1920 The Last Fortnight.
1922 Follow My Leader.
     Ancient Rome.
1923 The Man of Tomorrow.
1924 Mary Macarthur.
     J. Ramsay MacDonald   (*Reissued* 1929.)
1925 Margaret Bondfield.
1926 Thomas Carlyle.
     Greece.
1927 Folly's Handbook.
1930 Three Against Fate.
1932 Murder in the House of Commons.
     In America Today.
1933 Beatrice and Sidney Webb.
     John Stuart Mill.
1935 Sentenced to Life.

BOOKS BY JOHN LIVINGSTON LOWES

1919 Convention and Revolt in Poetry.
1927 The Road to Xanadu.
1930 Of Reading Books.
1931 The Art of Geoffrey Chaucer.
1934 Geoffrey Chaucer.

BOOKS BY ARCHIBALD MacLEISH

1917 Tower of Ivory.
1924 The Happy Marriage.
1925 The Pot of Earth.
1926 Nobodaddy.
     Streets in the Moon. (*Reissued* 1928.)
1928 The Hamlet of A. MacLeish.

1930	New Found Land.
1932	Conquistador.
1933	Frescoes for Mr. Rockefeller's City.
	Selected Poems.
1935	Panic.

BOOKS BY GEORGE FORT MILTON

| 1931 | The Age of Hate: Andrew Johnson and the Radicals. |
| 1934 | The Eve of Conflict: Stephen A. Douglas and the Needless War. |

BOOKS BY HAROLD NICOLSON

1920	Paul Verlaine.
1921	Sweet Waters.
1923	Tennyson.
1924	Byron: The Last Journey.
1925	Swinburne.
1927	Some People. (*Reissued* 1934.)
1928	Development of English Biography.
1930	Portrait of a Diplomatist.
1933	Peacemaking 1919.
	Public Faces.
1934	Curzon: The Last Phase.
1935	Dwight Morrow.

BOOKS AND ANTHOLOGIES BY EDWARD J. O'BRIEN

1917	Poets of the Irish Revolutionary Brotherhood. (With Padraic Colum.)
	White Fountains.
1918	The Masque of Poets.
1919	The Forgotten Threshold.
	The Great Modern English Short Stories.
1921	Distant Music.

1923 The Advance of the American Short Story. (*Reissued* 1931.)
1927 Hard Sayings.
1929 The Dance of the Machines.
1930 Modern English Short Stories.
1931 The Twenty-Five Finest Short Stories.
1932 Son of the Morning: A Life of Nietzsche.
     Modern American Short Stories.
1934 English Short Stories of Today.
1935 New English Short Stories.
     The Guest Book.
     The Short Story Case Book.
1915–35 The Best Short Stories. 21 annual volumes.
1922–25 The Best British Short Stories. (With John Cournos.) 4 annual volumes.
1926–35 The Best British Short Stories. 10 annual volumes.

BOOKS BY E. ARNOT ROBERTSON

1928 Cullum.
1930 Three Came Unarmed.
1931 Four Frightened People.
1933 Ordinary Families.

BOOKS BY RAFAEL SABATINI

1904 The Tavern Knight. (*Reissued* 1927.)
1906 Bardleys the Magnificent. (*Reissued* 1924).
     Trampling of the Lilies. (*Reissued* 1925.)
1907 Love at Arms. (*Reissued* 1925.)
1908 The Shame of Motley. (*Reissued* 1925.)
1909 St. Martin's Summer. (*Reissued* 1924.)
1910 Arms and the Maid. (*Reissued* 1924 as Mistress Wilding.)
1911 The Lion's Skin. (*Reissued* 1926.)
1912 Cesare Borgia. (*Reissued* 1924.)
1913 Torquemada. (*Reissued* 1924.)
     The Strolling Saint. (*Reissued* 1925.)

1914 The Gates of Doom. (*Reissued* 1925.)
1915 The Sea-Hawk. (*Reissued* 1923.)
1917 The Banner of the Bull. (*Reissued* 1923.)
      The Snare. (*Reissued* 1923.)
1918 Historical Nights' Entertainment, Vol. I. (*Reissued* 1924.)
1919 Historical Nights' Entertainment, Vol. II. (*Reissued* 1924.)
1921 Scaramouche.
1922 Captain Blood.
1923 Fortune's Fool.
1925 The Carolinian.
1926 Bellarion.
1927 The Nuptials of Corbal.
1928 The Hounds of God.
1929 The Romantic Prince.
1930 The King's Minion.
1931 Captain Blood Returns.
      Scaramouche, the King-Maker.
1932 The Black Swan.
1933 The Stalking Horse.
1934 Heroic Lives.
      Venetian Masque.
1935 Chivalry.

BOOKS BY FRANCES LESTER WARNER

1919 Endicott and I.
1921 Pilgrim Trails.
      Life's Minor Collisions. (With Gertrude C. Warner.)
1923 Groups and Couples.
1925 Steel and Holly.
1926 Surprising the Family.
1928 The Unintentional Charm of Men.
1929 To the People we Like.
1933 Pleasures and Palaces. (With Gertrude C. Warner.)

BOOKS BY VALENTINE WILLIAMS

- 1918 The Man with the Clubfoot. (*Reissued* 1931.)
- 1919 The Secret Hand.
- 1922 The Yellow Streak.
- 1923 The Orange Divan. (*Reissued* 1931.)
  Island Gold.
- 1924 The Three of Clubs.
  Clubfoot the Avenger.
- 1925 The Red Mass.
- 1926 Mr. Ramosi.
  The Key Man.
- 1927 The Eye in Attendance.
- 1928 The Crouching Beast.
- 1930 The Knife Behind the Curtain.
  The Mysterious Miss Morrisot.
- 1932 The Mystery of the Gold Box.
  Death Answers the Bell.
- 1933 The Clock Ticks On.
  Fog. (With Dorothy Rice Sims.)
- 1934 The Portcullis Room.
  Masks off at Midnight.
- 1935 The Clue of the Rising Moon.

VIRGINIA WOOLF

For there is something, Fanny thought, about books which if I had been educated I could have liked.

CERVANTES

There is no book so bad but something good may be found in it.

FRANK SWINNERTON

To read a book once is like meeting a man once — and never again.

CHARLES LAMB

I can read anything which I call a book... and I bless my stars for a taste so catholic, so unexcluding.

CICERO

To add a library to a house is to give that house a soul.

RUSKIN

If a book is worth reading, it is worth buying.